Directory of Publishing
in Scotland
1997

Scottish Publishers Association
Edinburgh

First published in 1988

Sixth edition published in 1997 by:
Scottish Publishers Association
Scottish Book Centre
137 Dundee Street
Edinburgh
EH11 1BG

British Library Cataloguing in Publication Data
A record for this book is available from the British Library

ISBN 0 9513912 4 0

THE SCOTTISH **ARTS** COUNCIL

Cover design by Janet Watson, Glasgow, 0141 550 4994
Cover photograph by McCandlish & Robson, Kirkintilloch, 0141 777 7900
Printed and bound in the UK by The Cromwell Press from Postscript disk,
    direct to plate on 100gsm Cromwell Educational Wove

CONTENTS

Services

Writing

INTRODUCTION

Each day, the Scottish Publishers Association (known as the SPA) receives enquiries about books and publishing in Scotland and about the practicalities of an increasingly complex book business. This directory was designed not simply as a reference point for booksellers and publishers, but also as a source of information to answer many of those enquiries, to be used by authors and illustrators, designers, printers, consultants, freelancers and by the public in general. Many specialist books exist which give information on the specific skills, issues and topics of the book trade, a selection of which are listed here in the bibliography, but in compiling the *Directory of Publishing in Scotland*, the SPA's priority has been to assemble and highlight the information on and for Scotland. The first edition of this directory was produced in 1988. This is the sixth, expanded edition.

The arrangement of the *Directory* has been altered slightly, in an attempt to make the main sections more concise and comprehensive. The 'Publishing' section now includes publishing notes and contacts as well as information on publishing training establishments. The final section has been re-named 'Writing' and includes a wealth of information for both the aspiring and the established writer. The 'Organisations' section has, again, been expanded to include more contacts. If you feel your organisation should be listed here, please let the SPA know.

The companies and individuals listed here have all offered themselves for inclusion when we called for information in June 1996 and it is hoped that the list gives a fair representation of services available in Scotland to anyone connected with or interested in the book trade.

As ever, the SPA welcomes suggestions for items to be included in future editions of the *Directory of Publishing in Scotland* and asks that changes and amendments to the entries be notified as soon as possible (*please see form on p. 127*). All information is correct at the time of going to press.

ACKNOWLEDGEMENTS

In compiling this volume, the Scottish Publishers Association is grateful for the help of all the people who supplied information about the various comapanies, groups and organisations listed. Thanks also go to all freelancers who submitted entries for the service section.

The Scottish Publishers Association would also like to thank The Cromwell Press, printers of the *Directory*, for their continued support of this publication.

PUBLISHING

SCOTTISH PUBLISHERS ASSOCIATION

Scottish Book Centre, 137 Dundee Street, Edinburgh EH11 1BG
Tel: 0131 228 6866
Fax: 0131 228 3220
Date established: 1974
Contacts: Lorraine Fannin (Director); Davinder Bedi
(Administrator); Susanne Gilmour (Publicity and Marketing
Manager); Joanna Mattinson (Scottish Book Marketing Group and
Promotions); Allan Shanks (Projects Assistant)
Services offered: Information, promotion, publicity and marketing
services, advice and consultancy, training. See over, under 'Aims'
for a fuller description of SPA services to members.

―――――――――――**Background**―――――――――――

Two hundred years ago, at the end of the eighteenth century and
for the early years of the nineteenth, Edinburgh challenged
London as the print capital of the world. In the space of a few
decades, some of the most illustrious names in publishing
emerged and flourished, reflecting the intellectual optimism of
the Enlightenment in Scotland and Sir Walter Scott's phenomenal
popularity at home and on the Continent.

Firms like Archibald Constable (once called the Edinburgh
University Press) and William Blackwood, whose influence
through their respective periodicals, *Edinburgh Review* and
Blackwood's Magazine, extended worldwide and were in the
forefront of a publishing explosion. Others followed quickly at
their heels: Thomas Nelson, A. & C. Black, Blackie & Son,
W. & R. Chambers, William Collins, Oliver & Boyd,
Bartholomew and T. & T. Clark all carved a niche for themselves
in a competitive market-place, contributing to Edinburgh's boast
of being a city built on beer, biscuits and books.

Publishing and printing were often carried out by the same
company (though in more recent years this has become an
obsolete practice). Booksellers were often publishers as well.
Over the course of the nineteenth century, however, the power
centre gradually shifted back towards London. Some Scottish
firms opened offices in the south, merged or expanded into
conglomerates, Scottish in name only. By the 1960s several large
Scottish publishers were still engaged in general publishing,
though many more had passed into the ownership of multinationals
which now control what was once a family-dominated industry. By

the beginning of the 1970s, though, it was clear that some change was under way; new companies were springing up and Scottish writing was flourishing.

Around 40 small presses were extant in 1974, the same year that the Scottish Publishers Association (SPA) was formed. The original group, known as the Scottish General Publishers Association, was formed by 12 publishers. The first chairman was Robin Lorimer, shortly followed by Norman Wilson, who worked with the other members to secure Scottish Arts Council support for this initiative, funding which remains a continuing lifeline.

The SPA has now become much more complex with a full programme of international marketing, services and promotions. It still provides the element of mutual help and advice which members share with each other, recognising a common purpose in a time of difficulty for the whole industry and combining all possible resources to bring Scottish-published books to the attention of the reading public.

Aims

The Scottish Publishers Association aims to help publishing concerns in Scotland to conduct their book publishing businesses in a professional manner, to market their output to the widest possible readership within Scotland, the UK and overseas and to encourage the development of a literary culture in Scotland.

A programme of activities is planned annually which provides a range of opportunity to all publishers, whatever their size, scope, speciality or geographical location. These activities are offered on a cooperative basis in order to save costs and administrative time. In outline they consist of: attendance at book fairs – home and abroad; marketing to bookshops, schools and libraries; publicity and advertising services; provision of professional training facilities in publishing skills, information resources and consultancy.

In addition the SPA implements research, develops projects and liaises with outside organisations which are considered to be of interest and benefit to the membership of the SPA, for example with Book House Training Centre, with universities in providing publishing education, with The British Council and International Book Development.

The resources with which the SPA carries out these objectives include staff expertise, the premises and facilities of the Scottish

Book Centre (*see p. 62*), financial assistance from the Scottish Arts Council, subscriptions from members and annual earnings from services offered. These resources are constantly developed to bring improved benefit to the membership.

Membership is open to all companies and organisations in Scotland who publish books for sale. Aspiring members should have published at least two books, whose authors should be other than the principals of the company. There should also be a commitment to a future publishing programme. Associate Membership is open to those concerns whose aims and aspirations are compatible with those of the SPA and who may be thought to derive benefit from the Association, although they may not have fulfilled the membership criteria. Associate members are not eligible for nomination to the Council of the SPA, this Council being elected annually by and from the membership.

The following services are offered to all members of the SPA:

- A quarterly newsletter with marketing, trade fair, employment, manuscript, bookshop, overseas and general publishing information.
- Information, advice and access to the SPA reference and resource library.
- Access to services provided by International Book Development who help with export initiative queries and provide an export newsletter for subscribing members, Department of Trade and Industry (DTI) information on British/Scottish promotions abroad and advertising opportunities overseas.

Other services offered are charged at low rates. They include:

- Advance information mailing and catalogue mailings to all major bookshops, wholesalers, library suppliers, press and media contacts in Scotland and to major media contacts in London.
- Spring and autumn new books brochures which are distributed via the SPA mailings to the UK book trade, media, school resource centres, universities, school libraries, wholesalers, book clubs, library suppliers, all British Councils and a number of overseas customers. The leaflet is also used as promotional material at SPA displays, trade fairs and conferences.
- Mailing list labels from an extensive and regularly-updated database.

• Representation at book fairs in the UK and abroad. Members may display their books on the SPA stand even if they do not attend the fair personally. The fairs attended are:

London International Book Fair
Booksellers Association Conference
BookExpo America (formerly the American Booksellers Association Convention)
Australian Book Fair
Frankfurt Book Fair
The Edinburgh Book Festival
Scottish Library Association Conference
Schoolbook exhibitions and many others

- Promotional activities include joint advertising, press and media campaigns, book display facilities, Scottish Book Marketing Group promotions such as Scottish Book Fortnight and a summer tourist promotion (*see p. 43*). In addition, the publicist is available to assist members in planning individual press and publicity campaigns.
- Training in aspects of publishing, seminars on current publishing issues.
- Export sales consortium to facilitate overseas sales.

The SPA held its first conference in Perth in 1996. Over the one-and-a-half days, booksellers, librarians and publishers met to discuss the industry in general, specific topics (such as electronic publishing, copyright and contracts) and to share ideas in an informal setting. It is hoped that a further Conference will take place in June 1997 and that the event will, thereafter, take place every second year.

Scottish Publishers Association Members
Full Members

ACAIR LTD

7 James Street, Stornoway, Isle of Lewis HS1 2QN
Tel: 01851 703020
Fax: 01851 703294
ISBNs and imprints: 0 86152
Company established: 1977
Titles in print: 291
Contacts: Donalda MacLeod; Hugh Andrew (Sales) 14 High Street, Edinburgh EH1 1TE. Tel/fax: 0131 558 1500
Types of books published: All categories of fiction and non-fiction for children in the Gaelic language. Adult books relating to the Gaidhealtachd, history, music, poetry, biography, environmental studies, Gaelic language.
Distributor: Scottish Book Source, 137 Dundee Street, Edinburgh EH11 1BG. Tel: 0131 229 6800. Fax: 0131 299 9070.

AK PRESS

PO Box 12766, Edinburgh EH8 9YE
Tel: 0131 555 5165
Fax: 0131 555 5215
E-mail: ak@akedin.demon.co.uk
ISBNs and imprints: 1 873176
Company established: 1991
Titles in print: 52
Contact: Alexis McKay (Editorial, Sales)
Types of books published: Politics, philosophy, critical theory, history, graphic art, fiction, ecology, media
Distributor: AK Distribution

AMAISING PUBLISHING HOUSE LTD, THE

Unit 7, Greendykes Industrial Estate, Greendykes Road, Broxburn, West Lothian EH52 6PG
Tel: 01506 857570
Fax: 01506 858100
ISBNs and imprints: 1 87512
Company established: 1987
Titles in print: 24
Contacts: Katrena Allan (Managing Director); Gordon Allan (Operations Director); Norma Rutherford (Sales, Marketing); Dena Brookfield (Accounts)
Types of books published: Children's illustrated
Distributor: The Amaising Publishing House Ltd

APPLETREE PRESS LTD

Aquarius House, 80–82 Chiswick High Road, London
W4 1SY
Tel: 0181 987 9439
Fax: 0181 987 9443
E-mail: 100407.1304@compuserve.com
ISBNs and imprints: 0 86281
Company established: 1974
Titles in print: 180
Contact: David Ross (Marketing Director)
Types of books published: Gift and information books
Distributor: Scottish Book Source, 137 Dundee Street, Edinburgh
EH11 1BG. Tel: 0131 229 6800. Fax: 0131 229 9070

ARGYLL PUBLISHING

Glendaruel, Argyll PA22 3AE
Tel/fax: 01369 820229
ISBNs and imprints: 1 874640
Company established: 1992
Titles in print: 45
Contact: Derek Rodger (Proprietor)
Types of books published: General titles including health, sport,
biography, politics and fiction
Distributor: Biblios Publishers Distribution Sevices Ltd, Star Road,
Partridge Green, West Sussex, RH13 8LD. Tel: 01403 710971. Fax:
01403 711143 (England only); Bookspeed, Edinburgh

ASSOCIATION FOR SCOTTISH LITERARY STUDIES

c/o Dept of Scottish History, University of Glasgow,
9 University Gardens, Glasgow G12 8QH
Tel: 0141 330 5309
E-mail: cmc@arts.gla.ac.uk
ISBNs and imprints: 0 948877
Company established: 1970
Titles in print: 36 plus journals
Contact: Catherine McInerney (Manager)
Types of books published: Works of Scottish literature which have
either been neglected or which need to be presented afresh to a
contemporary audience; anthologies of new Scottish writing in
English, Gaelic and Scots; essays and monographs on the literature
and languages of Scotland; comprehensive study guides to major
Scottish writers.
Distributor: Scottish Book Source, 137 Dundee Street, Edinburgh
EH11 1BG. Tel: 0131 229 6800. Fax: 0131 229 9070. (ASLS
members order direct from ASLS)

ATELIER BOOKS

6 Dundas Street, Edinburgh EH3 6HZ
Tel: 0131 557 4050
Fax: 0131 557 8382
ISBNs and imprints: 0 951 and 1 873830
Company established: 1987
Titles in print: 5
Contacts: Patrick Bourne (Director); Fiona Drennan
Types of books published: Books on art and artists
Distributor: Atelier Books

B&W PUBLISHING LTD

233 Cowgate, Edinburgh EH1 1NQ
Tel: 0131 220 5551
Fax: 0131 220 5552
ISBNs and imprints: 0 951515 and 1 873631
Company established: 1990
Titles in print: 60
Contact: Campbell Brown
Types of books published: Fiction, memoirs, guide books, general
Distributor: B&W Publishing Ltd

BIRLINN LTD

14 High Street, Edinburgh EH1 1TE
Tel: 0131 556 6660
Fax: 0131 558 1500
ISBNs and imprints: 1 874744 and 1 899272
Company established: 1992
Titles in print: 62
Contact: Hugh Andrew (Editorial, Sales, Publicity)
Types of books published: Scottish classics and humour, local
interest, Gaelic, West Coast
Distributor: Scottish Book Source, 137 Dundee Street, Edinburgh
EH11 1BG. Tel: 0131 229 6800. Fax: 0131 229 9070

BLACK ACE BOOKS

Ellemford Farmhouse, Duns, Berwickshire TD11 3SG
Tel: 01361 890370
Fax: 01361 890287
ISBNs and imprints: 1 872988
Company established: 1992
Titles in print: 16
Contacts: Hunter Steele (Editorial, Production); Boo Wood (Sales,
Publicity)
Types of books published: Non-fiction; new fiction, primarily by
Scottish authors; paperback reprints of quality fiction
Distributor: Black Ace Books

BROWN, SON & FERGUSON, LTD

4–10 Darnley Street, Glasgow G41 2SD
Tel: 0141 429 1234 (24 hrs)
Fax: 0141 420 1694
ISBNs and imprints: 0 85174
Company established: *c*. 1850
Titles in print: Over 500
Contacts: L. Ingram-Brown (Joint Managing Director);
D. H. Provan (Sales Manager)
Types of books published: Nautical and yachting, sea literature,
ship's stationery, nautical magazine, drama, poetry, Scout and Guide
books
Distributor: Brown, Son & Ferguson, Ltd

CANONGATE BOOKS

14 High Street, Edinburgh EH1 1TE
Tel: 0131 557 5111
Fax: 0131 557 5211
E-mail: canon.gate@almac.co.uk
ISBNs and imprints: 0 86241 Canongate Books, Canongate
Classics, Canongate Kelpies, Payback Press; 1 85968 Canongate
Audio; 1 56656 Interlink Books (USA); 0 86241 Rebel Inc.
Company established: 1994 (under present name)
Titles in print: 200
Contacts: Jamie Byng (Joint Managing Director); Hugh Andrew
(Joint Managing Director, Sales)
Types of books published: General interest, Scottish, fiction, music,
Afro-American literature, poetry, art, history, biography, reference,
children's fiction, audio cassettes
Distributor: Scottish Book Source, 137 Dundee Street, Edinburgh
EH11 1BG. Tel: 0131 229 6800. Fax: 0131 229 9070

CHAPMAN

CHAPMAN

4 Broughton Place, Edinburgh EH1 3RX
Tel: 0131 557 2207
Fax: 0131 556 9565
ISBNs and imprints: 0 906772
Company established: 1970
Titles in print: 60
Contacts: Joy Hendry (Editorial); Sam Wood (Administration)
Types of books published: Literary magazine, poetry, fiction.
Chapman: Scotland's Quality Literary Magazine is the mainstay of
this small, dynamic publishing house. The imprint, 'Chapman
Publishing', developed out of the work of the magazine and has now
established itself as one of Scotland's most adventurous publishers
of poetry, as well as short stories and plays.
Distributor: Chapman

CHURCHILL LIVINGSTONE – Medical Division of Pearson Professional

Robert Stevenson House, 1–3 Baxter's Place, Edinburgh EH1 3AF

CHURCHILL LIVINGSTONE

Tel: 0131 556 2424
Fax: 0131 558 1278
E-mail: *first name and first initial of surname*@edinburgh.rsh.pearson-pro.com
ISBNs and imprints: 0 443
Company established: 1724
Titles in print: 1,500
Contacts: Andrew Stevenson (Managing Director); Peter Shepherd (Director, Medical Education and Nursing and Allied Health); John Richardson (Publishing Services Director); Peter Richardson (Director, Health Care Information and Management); Timothy Wright (Sales Director); Susan Jerdan-Taylor (Marketing Manager); Eileen Horne (Human Resources Director); Rita Scheman (Vice President, Periodicals/Multimedia)
Types of books published: All areas of health science, including medicine, nursing, physiotherapy, dentistry, complementary medicine
Distributor: Southport Book Distributors

EDINBURGH CITY LIBRARIES

Central Library, George IV Bridge, Edinburgh EH1 1EG
Tel: 0131 225 5584
Fax: 0131 225 8783
ISBNs and imprints: 0 900353
Company established: 1890
Titles in print: 3
Contact: Bill Wallace (Head of Central Library and Information Services)
Types of books published: Books, booklets, prints, greetings cards

EDINBURGH PROJECT ON EXTENSIVE READING (EPER)

University of Edinburgh, 21 Hill Place, Edinburgh EH8 9OP
Tel: 0131 650 8211/6200
Fax: 0131 667 5927
ISBNs and imprints: 1 871914
Company established: 1987
Titles in print: 3
Contact: Mr D. R. Hill
Types of books published: Teaching guides to organising programmes in extensive reading, reading cards for learners of English as a foreign language (beginners and elementary)
Distributor: IALS, University of Edinburgh

EDINBURGH UNIVERSITY PRESS

22 George Square, Edinburgh EH8 9LF
Tel: 0131 650 4218
Fax: 0131 662 0053
E-mail: university.press@ed.ac.uk
ISBNs and imprints: 0 7486 and 0 85224
Company established: 1948 EUP; 1992 EUP Ltd
Titles in print: 500 plus 18 journals
Contacts: David Martin (Chairman); Ian Davidson (Production Director); Jackie Jones (Editorial Director); Keith Wright (Finance Director); Alison Munro (Marketing Director); Pamela O'Connor (Journals Manager)
Types of books published: Academic titles in Islamic studies, history, literature, linguistics, anthropology, philosophy, religious studies, sociology and women's studies. General titles in Scottish archaeology, architecture, history and literature.
Distributor: Marston Book Services Ltd, PO Box 269, Abingdon, Oxon OX14 4YN

See p. 23 for details of Polygon, affiliated to Edinburgh University Press

FINDHORN PRESS

The Park, Findhorn, Forres IV36 0TZ
Tel: 01309 690582
Fax: 01309 690036
E-mail: thierry@findhorn.org
Internet: http://www.mcn.org/findhorn/press/
ISBNs and imprints: 0 905249 and 1 899171
Company established: 1971
Titles in print: 50
Contacts: Karin and Thierry Bogliolo
Types of books published: New Age, from the Findhorn Foundation; also self-development, ecological, healing, humour
Distributor: Deep Books, Unit 13, Cannon Wharf Business Centre, 35 Evelyn Street, London SE8 5RT

FLORIS BOOKS

15 Harrison Gardens, Edinburgh EH11 1SH
Tel: 0131 337 2372
Fax: 0131 346 7516
E-mail: floris@edinburgh.net.uk
ISBNs and imprints: 0 86315 and 0 903540
Company established: 1977
Titles in print: 185
Contacts: Christian Maclean (Manager); Christopher Moore (Editor); Suzie Tombs (Sales)
Types of books published: Celtic studies; science; education; mind, body and spirit; religion; craft and activity; children's
Distributor: Floris Books. Also distributor for Lindisfarne Press

FORTH NATURALIST AND HISTORIAN

The University of Stirling, Stirling FK9 4LA   *the Forth*
and 30 Dunmar Drive, Alloa FK10 2EH   *Naturalist*
Tel: 01259 215091   *andHistorian*
Fax: 01786 464994
Telex: 777557 STUNIV G
E-mail: dsm2@stirling.ac.uk
ISBNs and imprints: 0 950696, 0 951414, 1 898008; ISSN 0309 7560
Company established: 1975
Titles in print: 18 volumes of an annual journal; 24, 1890s maps
with historical notes; 9 books; some 20 pamphlets
Contact: L. Corbett (Honorary Editor/Secretary)
Types of books published: Environment, heritage, wildlife – papers
and reviews in the annual *Forth Naturalist and Historian* – 1890s
maps with historical notes, commissioned for 24 places in central
Scotland jointly with Godfrey Maps of Newcastle.
Distributor: Forth Naturalist and Historian, University of Stirling

GEDDES & GROSSET LTD   **Geddes+**
Grosset

David Dale House, New Lanark, Lanark ML11 9DB
Tel: 01555 665000
Fax: 01555 665694
ISBNs and imprints: 1 85534
Company established: 1987
Titles in print: Own imprint: 140; packaged titles: 150; joint with
Time-Life: 120
Contacts: David Geddes; Ron Grosset; Mike Miller
Types of books published: Publishers and packagers of reference
books of all kinds, children's picture and story books, cookery
books, paperback classics, calendars and books as premiums and
promotional items.
Distributor: Geddes & Grosset Ltd, 32 Finlas Street, Glasgow G22 5DU

GLASGOW CITY LIBRARIES PUBLICATIONS BOARD

The Mitchell Library, North Street, Glasgow G3 7DN
Tel: *See contacts below*
Fax: 0141 287 2815   GLASGOW CITY LIBRARIES
ISBNs and imprints: 0 906169
Company established: 1980
Titles in print: 15 with 1 as co-publisher and more than 20 library
bibliographies
Contacts: J. Meighan (Editorial). Tel: 0141 287 2805;
V. Litster (Sales, Publicity). Tel: 0141 287 2846.
Types of books published: Mainly Glasgow interest or related to
material held in the Mitchell Library.
Distributor: The Mitchell Library

GLASGOW ROYAL CONCERT HALL, THE

2 Sauchiehall Street, Glasgow G2 3NY
Tel: 0141 332 6633
Fax: 0141 353 4150

THE GLASGOW ROYAL CONCERT HALL

ISBNs and imprints: 0 95221
Company established: 1990
Titles in print: 5
Contact: Alan S. Glen
Type of books published: Scottish transport history
Distributor: The Glasgow Royal Concert Hall

W. GREEN – The Scottish Law Publisher

21 Alva Street, Edinburgh EH2 4PS
Tel: 0131 225 4879
Fax: 0131 225 2104
E-mail: enquiries@wgreen.co.uk

W. GREEN
The Scottish Law Publisher

ISBNs and imprints: 0 414
Company established: 1734
Titles in print: 50
Contacts: Anthony Kinahan (Managing Director); Gilly Michie
(Marketing Manager); Vicki McGee (Sales); Maureen Marton
(Sales)
Type of books published: Scots law
Distributor: International Thomson Publishing Services

HARPERCOLLINS PUBLISHERS   ▦ HarperCollins*Publishers*

Westerhill Road, Bishopbriggs, Glasgow G64 2QT
Tel: 0141 772 3200   **Fax**: 0141 306 3119
and 77–81 Fulham Palace Road, London W6 8JB
Tel: 0181 307 4000   **Fax**: 0181 307 4440
ISBNs and imprints: 0 00
Company established: 1819
Titles in print: 10,000
Contacts: David Taylor (Group Sales Director, Scotland); Katharine
Toseland (Marketing, London); David Rye (Production Director);
Christopher Riches (Editorial Director, Reference, Glasgow)
Types of books published: General fiction, non-fiction, biography,
history, dictionaries and reference, children's, religious including
bibles, educational, sport, travel, home and leisure, cartographic
Distributor: HarperCollins, Bishopbriggs

HEALTH EDUCATION BOARD FOR SCOTLAND

Health Education Board for Scotland

Woodburn House, Canaan Lane, Edinburgh EH10 4SG
Tel: 0131 447 8044
Fax: 0131 452 8140
Company established: 1991
Titles in print: 91
Contacts: Alistair Craik (Publishing Manager); Sandra Watson (Production)
Types of books published: Health education, health promotion leaflets for the public; training and reference material for health professionals
Distributor: Health Education Board for Scotland

HOUSE OF LOCHAR

Isle of Colonsay, Argyll PA61 7YR
Tel/fax: 01951 200232
ISBNs and imprints: 1 899863
Company established: 1995
Titles in print: 32
Contacts: Kevin Byrne (Director); Georgina Hobhouse (Editorial, Sales); Grant Shipcott (Production)
Types of books published: Scottish interest, history, art, transport, topography
Distributor: House of Lochar

LAROUSSE PLC

LAROUSSE

7 Hopetoun Crescent, Edinburgh EH7 4AY
Tel: 0131 556 5929   **Fax**: 0131 556 5313
and 24 Great Titchfield Street, London W1P 7AD
Tel: 0171 631 0878   **Fax**: 0171 323 4694
ISBNs and imprints: 0 550 Chambers; 0 245 Harrap; 0 7523 Larousse; 0 86272 and 1 85697 Kingfisher
Company established: Chambers 1819; Larousse 1993
Titles in print: 2,000
Contacts: John Clement (Chairman); Maurice Shepherd (Director of Chambers Harrap Publishing and Pre-Press Operations); Robert Snuggs (Sales and Marketing Director); Tim Horsler (Business Development Director); Elaine Higgleton (Chambers Publishing Manager); Katharine Coates (Harrap Publishing Manager)
Types of books published: English and bilingual dictionaries, English usage, modern languages, general reference, academic, Scottish interest. Children's: fiction and non-fiction, natural history, general reference, encyclopedias and games.
Distributor: Macmillan Distribution, Brunnel Road, Houndmills, Basingstoke RG21 2XS. Tel: 01256 29242

LOMOND BOOKS

36 West Shore Road, Granton, Edinburgh EH5 1QD
Tel: 0131 551 2261
Fax: 0131 552 1703

L OMOND BOOKS

Company established: 1982
Titles in print: 16
Contacts: Trevor Maher (Sales); John Abernathy (Production, Editorial)
Types of books published: Scottish titles – mainly history, food and drink, photographic and guide books
Distributor: Lomond Books

LYLE PUBLICATIONS LTD

LYLE

Glenmayne, Galashiels, Selkirkshire TD1 3NR
Tel: 01896 752005
Fax: 01896 754696
ISBNs and imprints: 0 86248
Company established: 1969
Titles in print: 16
Contacts: Tony Curtis (Editorial); John Masters (Sales); Eelin McIvor (Publicity); Donna Rutherford (Distribution)
Types of books published: Price guides to antiques and collectables
Distributor: Lyle Publications

MAINSTREAM PUBLISHING

MAINSTREAM
PUBLISHING

7 Albany Street, Edinburgh EH1 3UG
Tel: 0131 557 2959
Fax: 0131 556 8720
E-mail: 101464.537@compuserve.com
ISBNs and imprints: 1 85158 and 0 906391
Company established: 1978
Titles in print: *c*. 300
Contacts: Bill Campbell (Joint Managing Director); Peter MacKenzie (Joint Managing Director); Raymond Cowie (Sales Manager); John Beaton (Editorial Director); Neil Graham (Production Manager); Sharon Atherton (Publicity Manager)
Types of books published: General non-fiction, fiction, biography, autobiography, art, photography, health, sport
Distributor: Tiptree Book Services Ltd, St Luke's Chase, Tiptree, Colchester, Essex CO5 0SR. Tel: 01621 816362. Fax: 01621 819717.

MERCAT PRESS

at James Thin Ltd, 53–59 South Bridge, Edinburgh EH1 1YS
Tel: 0131 556 6743
Fax: 0131 557 8149
E-mail: james.thin.ltd@almac.co.uk
Web site: http://www.almac.co.uk/business-park/thin/thinhome.htm
ISBNs and imprints: 0 901824 and 1 873644; 0 800 (ex-Aberdeen University Press)
Company established: 1970
Titles in print: 300
Contacts: Tom Johnstone; Seán Costello; John Brown (Sales)
Types of books published: Non-fiction, Scottish interest, general and academic books
Distributor: Mercat Press

MERCHISTON PUBLISHING

Dept of Print Media, Publishing and Communication, Napier University, Craighouse Road, Edinburgh EH10 5LG
Tel: 0131 455 6171
Fax: 0131 455 6193
ISBNs and imprints: 0 9511
Company established: 1988
Titles in print: 7
Contact: Mairi Sutherland
Types of books published: Merchiston Publishing provides a realistic working environment for students on BA Publishing. It specialises in books on Scottish and general publishing.
Distributor: Merchiston Publishing

MORAY HOUSE PUBLICATIONS

Moray House Institute of Education, Holyrood Campus, Holyrood Road, Edinburgh EH8 8AQ
Tel: 0131 558 6398
Fax: 0131 558 3428
ISBNs and imprints: 0 901580 and 1 899795
Company established: 1990
Titles in print: 34
Contact: Alan Hunter
Types of books published: Educational resource materials, educational curriculum materials, Moray House Institute research findings
Distributor: Moray House Publications

NATIONAL GALLERIES OF SCOTLAND

Belford Road, Edinburgh EH4 3DR
Tel: 0131 556 8921
Fax: 0131 315 2963
ISBNs and imprints: 0 903148 and 0 903598
Titles in print: 90
Contact: Janis Adams (Editorial, Sales, Publicity, Distribution)
Types of books published: Art/photography books and catalogues
Distributor: Lund Humphries

NATIONAL LIBRARY OF SCOTLAND

George IV Bridge, Edinburgh EH1 1EW
Tel: 0131 226 4531/ 0131 459 4531
Fax: 0131 220 6662
E-mail: publications@nls.uk
ISBNs and imprints: 0 90222 and 1 87211
Company established: 1925
Titles in print: 50
Contacts: Publications Officer (Editorial, Publicity); Publications
Sales (Sales, Distribution)
Types of books published: Bibliographies, facsimiles, catalogues,
literary and historical books
Distributor: National Library of Scotland

NATIONAL MUSEUMS OF SCOTLAND PUBLISHING

Chambers Street, Edinburgh EH1 1JF
Tel: 0131 247 4186/4164
Fax: 0131 247 4012
E-mail: fhk@nms.ac.uk
ISBNs and imprints: 0 948636 Trustees of the National Museums
of Scotland
Company established: 1985 (under present name)
Titles in print: 67
Contacts: Jenni Calder (Head of Publications); Helen Kemp
(Editor); Liz Robertson (Production); Brian Pugh (Sales)
Types of books published: Trade; scholarly books on the following:
history, art, archaeology, science, technology, geology, ethnography
natural history; popular Scottish history and culture
Distributor: Scotland: Scottish Book Source, 137 Dundee Street,
Edinburgh EH11 1BG. Tel: 0131 229 6800. Fax: 0131 229 9070; UK
(except Scotland) and Europe: Gazelle Book Services Ltd; Australia:
Reg Tigwell Art Agencies; USA: Arthur Schwartz & Co. Inc.;
Canada: University of British Columbia

NEIL WILSON PUBLISHING LTD

Suite 303a, The Pentagon Centre, 36 Washington Street, Glasgow G3 8AZ
Tel: 0141 221 1117
Fax: 0141 221 5363
E-mail: nwp@cqm.co.uk
Web site: http://www.nwp.co.uk/
ISBNs and imprints: 1 897784
Company established: 1992
Titles in print: 40
Contacts: Neil Wilson; Seol Ltd (Sales – Scotland); Exel Logistics (Sales – excluding Scotland)
Types of books published: Scottish interest, food and drink, hillwalking, sport, biography, Scottish history, humour, Irish interest, true crime
Distributor: Exel Logistics Media Services Ltd, Christchurch House, Beaufort Court, Sir Thomas Longley Road, Medway City Estate, Rochester, Kent ME2 4FX. Tel: 01634 297123. Fax: 01634 298000

NEW IONA PRESS, THE

7 Drynie Terrace, Inverness IV2 4UP
Tel/fax: 01463 242384
ISBNs and imprints: 0 9516283
Company established: 1990
Titles in print: 9
Contact: Mairi MacArthur (Director)
Types of books published: Local and natural history of the Hebridean islands of Mull and Iona
Distributor: The New Iona Press

POLYGON

22 George Square, Edinburgh EH8 9LF
Tel: 0131 650 4689
Fax: 0131 662 0053
ISBNs and imprints: 0 7486 and 0 904919
Company established: 1969
Titles in print: 150
Contacts: Marion Sinclair (Editorial); Alice Stoakley (Production); Jeanie Scott (Marketing and Publicity)
Types of books published: New fiction and poetry, determinations series on Scottish political culture, Scottish oral history
Distributor: Marston Book Services Ltd, PO Box 269, Abingdon, Oxon OX14 4YN
Polygon is affiliated to Edinburgh University Press, see p. 16

POOKIE PRODUCTIONS LTD

12 Craighouse Avenue, Edinburgh EH10 5LN
Tel: 0131 447 6750
Fax: 0131 447 7372
ISBNs and imprints: 1 872885
Company established: 1989
Titles in print: 12
Contacts: Heather Bonning; Cherry Hope
Types of books published: Children's illustrated fiction
Distributor: Biblios Publishers Distribution Services Ltd, Star
Road, Partridge Green, West Sussex RH13 8LD. Tel: 01403 710971.
Fax: 01403 711143.

RAMSAY HEAD PRESS, THE

15 Gloucester Place, Edinburgh EH3 6EE
Tel/fax: 0131 225 5646
ISBNs and imprints: 0 902859 and 1 873921
Company established: 1968
Titles in print: 35
Contacts: Christine and Conrad Wilson (Editorial); Christine Wilson
(Sales, Advertising); M. K. Young (Accounts)
Types of books published: Scottish interest, autobiography,
biography, fiction, poetry, academic, art and architecture, language
books and literary criticism
Distributor: The Ramsay Head Press

RICHARD STENLAKE PUBLISHING

Ochiltree Sawmill, The Lade, Ochiltree, Ayrshire KA18 2NX
Tel/fax: 01290 423114
ISBNs and imprints: 1 872074
Company established: 1990
Titles in print: 75
Contacts: Richard Stenlake; Campbell McCutcheon and Oliver van
Helden (Editorial); David Pettigrew (Sales)
Types of books published: Local history, industrial history,
transport history (not just Scottish!)
Distributor: Richard Stenlake Publishing

RUTLAND PRESS, THE

15 Rutland Square, Edinburgh EH1 2BE
Tel: 0131 229 7545
Fax: 0131 228 2188
ISBNs and imprints: 1 873190, 0 9501462 RIAS; 0 70730
joint with Scottish Academic Press; 1 85158 joint with
Mainstream Publishing

PRESS

Company established: *c*. 1922
Titles in print: 29
Contacts: Helen Leng (Publishing Manager); John Pelan (Business
Development Manager, RIAS; Sales)
Types of books published: Illustrated architectural guides,
monographs, reference
Distributor: The Rutland Press

SAINT ANDREW PRESS

121 George Street, Edinburgh EH2 4YN
Tel: 0131 225 5722
Fax: 0131 220 3113
ISBNs and imprints: 0 7152 Saint Andrew Press;
0 86153 Church of Scotland
Company established: 1954
Titles in print: 164
Contacts: Lesley A. Taylor (Publishing Manager); Derek Auld
(Sales and Production Manager); Ian Dunnet (Distribution);
Kathleen Casey (Invoicing)
Types of books published: Church of Scotland related titles and
books for the wider Christian market, local interest and some general
Distributor: Saint Andrew Press. Also distributor of Wild Goose
Publications, Pathway Productions (audio–visual) and Church of
Scotland Stationery.

SALTIRE SOCIETY, THE

9 Fountain Close, 22 High Street, Edinburgh EH1 1TF
Tel: 0131 556 1836
Fax: 0131 557 1675
ISBNs and imprints: 0 854110, 0 863340 and 0 904265;
The Saltire Society, Saltire New Poetry
Society established: 1936
Titles in print: 33
Contacts: Hugh Andrew (Marketing, Sales) 14 High Street, Edinburgh
EH1 1TE. Tel/fax: 0131 558 1500; Thorbjörn Campbell (Editorial)
Gleniffer Place, 3 Miller Road, Ayr KA7 2AX. Tel/fax: 01292 262359;
Cunison Rankin (Committee Convener) 16 Camps Road, Carnock,
Dunfermline KY12 9JP. Tel: 01383 850344. Fax: 01383 852290.
Types of books published: Scottish and Gaelic interest, history, law,
current affairs, poetry, criticism, biography, short stories
Distributor: Scottish Book Source, 137 Dundee Street, Edinburgh
EH11 1BG. Tel: 0131 229 6800. Fax: 0131 229 9070

SCOTTISH COUNCIL FOR RESEARCH IN EDUCATION, THE

15 St John Street, Edinburgh EH8 8JR
Tel: 0131 557 2944
Fax: 0131 556 9454
E-mail: SCRE@ed.ac.uk
Web site: http://www.ed.ac.uk/~webscre
ISBNs and imprints: 0 947833, 1 873303 and 1 86003
Company established: 1928
Titles in print: 142
Contacts: Dave Gilhooly (Sales, Distribution, Marketing);
Rosemary Wake (Editorial); Joyce Corrigan (Sales enquiries)
Types of books published: Educational research
Distributor: The Scottish Council for Research in Education

SCOTTISH CHILDREN'S PRESS

Unit 14, Leith Walk Business Centre, 130 Leith Walk,
Edinburgh EH6 5DT
Tel: 0131 555 5950
Fax: 0131 555 5018
ISBNs and imprints: 1 899827
Contacts: Avril Gray (Editorial); Jill Dick (Production, Sales)
Company established: 1995
Titles in print: 35
Types of books published: Children's fiction and non-fiction and
teachers' resource material – all with Scottish content. Written in
Scots, Gaelic or English.
Distributor: Scottish Book Source, 137 Dundee Street, Edinburgh
EH11 1BG. Tel: 0131 229 6800. Fax: 0131 229 9070

Scottish Children's Press is affiliated to Scottish Cultural Press, see opposite

SCOTTISH CULTURAL PRESS

Unit 14, Leith Walk Business Centre, 130 Leith Walk,
Edinburgh EH6 5DT
Tel: 0131 555 5950
Fax: 0131 555 5018
ISBNs and imprints: 1 898218 Scottish Cultural Press; 1 899827
Scottish Children's Press
Company established: 1992
Titles in print: 60
Contact: Jill Dick (Editorial, Production, Sales)
Types of books published: Scottish history, literature, poetry,
traditional. Children's fiction and non-fiction (*see Scottish
Children's Press entry opposite*)
Distributor: Scottish Book Source, 137 Dundee Street, Edinburgh
EH11 1BG. Tel: 0131 229 6800. Fax: 0131 229 9070

SCOTTISH LIBRARY ASSOCIATION

Scottish Centre for Information and Library Services,
1 John Street, Hamilton ML3 7EU
Tel: 01698 458888
Fax: 01698 458899
ISBNs and imprints: 0 900649
Company established: 1908
Titles in print: 12
Contact: Honorary Publications Officer, Alan Reid, c/o Midlothian
Libraries, Library HQ, 2 Clerk Street, Loanhead, Midlothian EH20
9DR. Tel: 0131 440 2210. Fax: 0131 440 4635
Types of books published: Librarianship, bibliographies, Scottish
interest, local and national history
Distributor: Scottish Book Source, 137 Dundee Street, Edinburgh
EH11 1BG. Tel: 0131 229 6800. Fax: 0131 229 9070.

SCOTTISH NATURAL HERITAGE

**SCOTTISH
NATURAL
HERITAGE**

Battleby, Redgorton, Perth PH1 3EW
Tel: 01738 627921   **Fax**: 01738 827411
and 12 Hope Terrace, Edinburgh EH9 2AS
Tel: 0131 447 4784   **Fax**: 0131 446 2277
ISBNs and imprints: 1 85397
Company established: 1992
Titles in print: over 100
Contacts: Elaine Dunlop (Head of Publications); Fiona Arnott
(Publishing Executive)
Types of books published: Environment, natural heritage,
governmental, education, general nature interest
Distributor: Scottish Natural Heritage, Battleby, Redgorton, Perth
PH1 3EW

SCOTTISH RECORD OFFICE

HM General Register House, Edinburgh EH1 3YY
Tel: 0131 535 1314
Fax: 0131 535 1360
ISBNs and imprints: 1 870874
Titles in print: 23
Contact: Publications and Education Branch
Types of books published: General historical and educational
publications designed to make the holdings of the Scottish Record
Office more accessible to amateur and professional searchers alike
Distributor: Scottish Record Office

SCOTTISH
RECORD OFFICE
the national archives

SHETLAND TIMES LTD, THE

Prince Alfred Street, Lerwick, Shetland ZE1 0EP
Tel: 01595 693622
Fax: 01595 694637
ISBNs and imprints: 0 900662 and 1 898852
Company established: 1872
Titles in print: 30
Contacts: Robert Wishart (Managing Director); Beatrice Nisbet
(Publications Manager)
Types of books published: Local interest
Distributor: The Shetland Times Bookshop, 71–79 Commercial
Street, Lerwick, Shetland ZE1 0AJ. Tel: 01595 695531.
Fax: 01595 692897. E-mail: bookshop@shetland-times.co.uk

STATIONERY OFFICE, THE
(formerly HMSO Scotland)

20 South Gyle Crescent, Edinburgh EH12 9EB
Tel: 0131 479 3101
Fax: 0131 479 3145
ISBNs and imprints: 0 10 and 0 11
Company established: 1906
Titles in Print: 50,000
Contact: Dr Sue Hemmings (Head of Publications); Penny Clarke
(Editorial, Publicity); Derek Jackson (Bookshop Manager); Debbie
Watson (Sales)
Types of books published: Parliamentary and governmental
material, historical, tourist guide books, exhibition catalogues,
Scottish interest publications
Distributor: The Stationery Office

The Stationery
Office
SCOTLAND

THISTLE PRESS

Thistle*Press*

West Bank, Western Road, Insch, Aberdeenshire
AB52 6JR
Tel/fax: 01464 821053
E-mail: info@thistlepress.co.uk
Web site: http://www.thistlepress.co.uk
ISBNs and imprints: 0 952095
Company established: 1992
Titles in print: 6
Contacts: Angela Nicholson (Editorial, Sales); Keith Nicholson
(Production, Sales)
Types of books published: Scottish regional travel guides; local
history, archaeology and geology with Scottish content; general
Scottish interest; academic books on the environmental sciences.
Distributor: Thistle Press

TUCKWELL PRESS LTD

The Mill House, Phantassie, East Linton, East Lothian
EH40 3DG
Tel/fax: 01620 860164
ISBNs and imprints: 1 898410
Company established: 1994
Titles in print: 64
Contacts: John Tuckwell (Editorial); Neville Moir (Production); Val
Tuckwell (Sales)
Types of books published: History, biography, ethnology and
folklife studies, language, literature and literary criticism
Distributor: Scottish Book Source, 137 Dundee Street, Edinburgh
EH11 1BG. Tel: 0131 229 6800. Fax: 0131 229 9070

UNIT FOR THE STUDY OF GOVERNMENT IN SCOTLAND

Chisholm House, 1 Surgeon Square, High School
Yards, Edinburgh EH1 1LZ
Tel: 0131 650 2456
Fax: 0131 650 6345
ISBNs and imprints: 0 9660356
Company established: 1976
Titles in print: 17
Contacts: Dr Lindsay Paterson (Editorial); Mrs Lindsay Adams
(Production, Sales, Publicity)
Types of books published: Research and debate on social, political,
economic and cultural topics which might be of particular interest to
Scotland, also similarly placed small nations/regions throughout
Europe and beyond
Distributor: Unit for the Study of Government in Scotland

WHITTLES PUBLISHING

Roseleigh House, Harbour Road, Latheronwheel,
Caithness KW5 6DW
Tel: 01593 741240
Fax: 01593 741360
ISBNs and imprints: 1 870325
Company established: 1986
Titles in print: 22
Contacts: Dr Keith Whittles (Editorial, Sales, Publicity)
Types of books published: Civil engineering and surveying; science
(petroleum geology, chemical and materials technology); general
(especially maritime/nautical and Scottish)
Distributor: Scottish Book Source, 137 Dundee Street, Edinburgh
EH11 1BG. Tel: 0131 229 6800. Fax: 0131 229 9070

WILD GOOSE PUBLICATIONS

Unit 15, 6 Harmony Row, Govan, Glasgow G51 3BA
Tel: 0141 440 0985
Fax: 0141 440 2338
ISBNs and imprints: 0 947988
Company established: 1985
Titles in print: 44
Contact: Sarelle Reid (Managing Editor, Wild Goose Publications);
Derek Auld (Sales, Saint Andrew Press)
Types of books published: Religious, especially drama, music
(books and tapes) and other worship resources
Distributor: Saint Andrew Press, 121 George Street, Edinburgh EH2
4YN. Tel: 0131 225 5722. Fax: 0131 220 3113

BOOK TRUST SCOTLAND

Scottish Book Centre, 137 Dundee Street, Edinburgh
EH11 1BG
Tel: 0131 229 3663
Fax: 0131 228 4293
ISBNs and imprints: 1 901077
Company established: 1961
Titles in print: 7
Contacts: Lindsey Fraser (Director); Kathryn Ross (Assistant
Director); Chris Young (Administrator/Librarian); Janet Smyth
(Readiscovery Touring Co-ordinator)
Types of books published: Currently in print: *Off the Shelf – A Guide
to Scotland's Writers and Illustrators for Children* (new edition);
Radical Reading (new edition); *20th Century Scottish Classics*;
reading Perthshire; *reading Glasgow* – a guide to books and authors
associated with that city; *Wild About Books!* (poster); Scottish Poetry
Posters (new set of four); *Plug Into Books* (audio cassette – children's)
Distributor: Book Trust Scotland; Scottish Book Source, 137
Dundee Street, Edinburgh EH11 1BG. Tel: 0131 229 6800.
Fax: 0131 229 9070
See p. 57 for further information

GAELIC BOOKS COUNCIL, THE

22 Mansfield Street, Glasgow G11 5QP
Tel: 0141 337 6211
ISBNs and imprints: 0 951281
Company established: 1968
Titles in print: 1
Contact: Ian MacDonald
Types of books published: Catalogues and book news magazines;
poetry posters
Distributor: The Gaelic Books Council
See p. 61 for further information

GLENEIL PRESS, THE

Whittingehame, Haddington, East Lothian EH41 4QA
Tel/fax: 01620 860292
ISBNs and imprints: 0 952533
Company established: 1995
Titles in print: 4
Contacts: Michael Brander (Sales, Editorial)
Types of books published: Scottish interest: historical, biography,
sporting
Distributor: Scottish Book Source, 137 Dundee Street, Edinburgh
EH11 1BG. Tel: 0131 229 6800. Fax: 0131 229 9070

31

REED BOOKS

Michelin House, 81 Fulham Road, London SW3 6RB
Tel: 0171 581 9393
Fax: 0171 225 9424
ISBNs and imprints: 0 600 Hamlyn; 0 5400 Philip's; 1 85732 and 0
85533 Mitchell Beazley and Miller's; 1 85532 and 0 85045 Osprey;1
85619 Sinclair-Stevenson; 0 436 Secker & Warburg; 0 434
Heinemann; 0 413 and 0 416 Methuen; 0 7497 Mammoth;
1 85591 Buzz; 0 7493 Mandarin/Minerva; 1 85029 Conran Octopus;
1 85152 Bounty; 0 603 Dean
Titles in print: 10,000
Contacts: Alan Jessop (Group Sales Director); Vince Smith
(Production Director); Helen Fraser (Trade Editorial); Jane
Winterbotham (Children's Editorial); Laura Bamford (Hamlyn
Editorial); Jane Aspden (Mitchell Beazley Editorial); John Wallace
(Conran Octopus Editorial); Jonathon Parker (Osprey Editorial);
John Gaisford (Philips Editorial); Barney Allan (International Sales
Director)
Types of books published: All types
Distributor: Exel Logistics Media Services Ltd, Christchurch
House, Beaufort Court, Sir Thomas Longley Road, Medway City
Estate, Rochester, Kent ME2 4FX. Tel: 01634 297123. Fax: 01634
298000

ROYAL COMMISSION ON THE ANCIENT AND HISTORICAL MONUMENTS OF SCOTLAND

John Sinclair House, 16 Bernard Terrace, Edinburgh EH8 9NX
Tel: 0131 662 1456
Fax: 0131 662 1477/1499
Titles in print: 19
Contacts: Mr R. J. Mercer (Editorial); Mr John N. Stevenson
(Production); Mrs Carole Buglass (Sales)
Types of books published: Surveys of field material, both
archaeological and architectural; surveys and catalogues of material
held in National Monuments Record of Scotland.
Distributor: RCAHMS

SCOTTISH HOMES, RESEARCH AND INNOVATION SERVICE

Scottish Homes

Rosebery House, 9 Haymarket Terrace,
Edinburgh
EH12 5YA
Tel: 0131 313 0044
Fax: 0131 313 1115
Web site: http://www.scot-homes.gov.uk
ISBNs and imprints: 1 874170
Company established: 1989
Titles in print: Over 100
Contacts: Caitlin McCorry (Production, Editorial); Janette Campbell (Sales)
Types of books published: Research reports, precis, innovation studies, social reports, working papers. Also publishers of the journal, *Housing Research Review*.
Distributor: Scottish Homes

SCOTTISH MUSIC INFORMATION CENTRE

1 Bowmont Gardens, Glasgow G12 9LR
Tel: 0141 334 6393
Fax: 0141 337 1161
ISBNs and imprints: 0 95254
Company established: 1985
Titles in print: 1
Contact: Kirsteen McCue (General Manager)
Type of book published: *Scottish Music Handbook*
Distributor: Scottish Book Source, 137 Dundee Street, Edinburgh EH11 1BG. Tel: 0131 229 6800. Fax: 0131 229 9070

STRAIGHTLINE PUBLISHING LTD

29 Main Street, Bothwell, Glasgow G71 8RD
Tel: 01698 853000
Fax: 01698 854208

 STRAIGHTLINE PUBLISHING LTD

Company established: 1989
Titles in print: 7
Contacts: F. Docherty (Production); P. Bellew (Sales, Publicity)
Types of books published: Specialist facts books, Education Department projects, annual reports, *Institute Quarterly*, corporate newsletters
Distributor: Straightline Publishing Ltd

DUDU NSOMBA PUBLICATIONS
4 Gailes Park, Bothwell, Glasgow G71 8TS
Tel: 01698 854290
Fax: 01698 854472
ISBNs and imprints: 0 9522233
Company established: 1993
Contact: Dr John Lwanda
Types of books published: General, politics, children's stories, poetry, social science, especially relating to Malawi
Distributor: Dudu Nsomba Publications

FAMEDRAM
Mill Business Centre, PO Box 3, Ellon, Aberdeenshire AB41 9EA
Tel: 01651 842429
Fax: 01651 842180
E-mail: famedram@artwork.co.uk
ISBNs and imprints: 0 950194 and 0 905489 Northern Books
Company established: 1971
Contacts: Bill Williams and Eleanor Stewart
Types of books published: Local history, transport, Arts, football
Distributor: Various distributors

GORDON WRIGHT PUBLISHING LTD
25 Mayfield Road, Edinburgh EH9 2NQ
Tel: 0131 667 1300
Fax: 0131 667 1459
E-mail: 101370.330@compuserve.com
ISBNs and imprints: 0 903065
Company established: 1969
Contacts: Gordon Wright and Carmen Wright
Types of books published: General Scottish
Distributor: All orders and correspondence to the above address

HISTORICAL PRESS, THE
Megginch, Errol, Perth PH2 7SW
Tel: 01821 642 222
Fax: 01821 642 708
E-mail: 101355.1554
ISBNs and imprints: 1 871430
Company established: 1993
Types of books published: Reminiscenses, diaries of local or national/international interest
Distributor: The Historical Press

JOHN DONALD PUBLISHERS LTD

138 St Stephen Street, Edinburgh EH3 5AA
Tel: 0131 225 1146
Fax: 0131 220 0567
ISBNs and imprints: 0 85976
Company established: 1973
Contacts: D.L. Morrison (Publisher); J.G. Angus (Sales); J. Elder (Finance)
Types of books published: Academic, local history, Discovering Series
Distributor: John Donald Publishers Ltd

JOHNSTON & BACON BOOKS

PO Box 1, Stirling FK16 6BE
Tel: 01786 841330
Fax: 01786 841326
ISBNs and imprints: 0 7179 4
Company established: 1893
Contact: David Warburton
Types of books published: Local history, clans, cookery, guidebooks
Distributor: Clan Books Ltd, The Cross, Doune, Perthshire FK16 6BE

TETRAHEDRON BOOKS

30 Birch Crescent, Blairgowrie, Perthshire PH10 6TS
Tel: 01250 874397
ISBNs and imprints: 0 95198
Company established: 1992
Contact: Peter Mackie
Types of books published: Books for teenagers
Distributor: Tetrahedron Books

Publishing Notes and Contacts

The process of transforming a typescript into a book, a publication of quality, requires organisational skills and creative ideas together with a sound grasp of finance and a flair for marketing – a combination of talent and experience which is not easily perfected. There are key steps which each publisher must take, whatever the company's size, scope and organisation, and for those who have a small in-house team, the list of freelance services in this directory should be helpful (*see pp. 74–92 for listings*).

For those beginning in the business, however, a first step is to give books a professional image by ensuring that the basic publishing conventions are followed: it is essential to obtain an International Standard Book Number (ISBN), a bar code and to make available Cataloguing in Publication Data. It is also mandatory to acknowledge copyright and to deposit copies of the book in the copyright libraries.

ISBN

International Standard Book Numbering is the system of giving each book a unique ten-digit code which identifies that title (or one particular edition of the title) from one specific publisher. ISBNs are issued by:

STANDARD BOOK NUMBERING AGENCY LTD
12 Dyott Street,
London WC1A 1DF
Tel: 0171 420 6000   **Fax**: 0171 836 4342
See also p. 72

Bar codes

These allow the book's details to be read by electronic means at the point of sale in a bookshop (or at the issue desk in a library). Most bookshops use a system called Electronic Point of Sale (EPOS) which records each transaction and helps to manage the stock orders. Bar codes may be obtained from:

ALBAR CODING SERVICES
15 Thistle Street, Dunfermline, KY12 0JA
Tel/fax: 01383 737700
E-mail: 106132.2270@compuserve.com

Cataloguing in Publication Data

The British Library Cataloguing in Publication programme is a cooperative scheme involving British publishers and The British Library. Cataloguing in Publication Data (or CIP Data) is a block of cataloguing information, supplied to the publisher in order to aid libraries. Information about this scheme can be obtained from:

BIBLIOGRAPHIC DATA SERVICES LTD
24 Nith Place
Dumfries
DG1 2PN
Tel: 01387 266004   **Fax**: 01387 265503

Copyright libraries

Publishers in the UK and Ireland have a legal obligation to send one copy of each of their publications to the Legal Deposit Office of the British Library within one month of publication. Publications should be sent to:

LEGAL DEPOSIT OFFICE
The British Library,
Boston Spa, Wetherby
West Yorkshire LS23 7BY
Tel: 01937 546267   **Fax**: 01937 546176

Further copies must also be sent to the Bodleian Library, Oxford; University Library, Cambridge; the National Library of Scotland; the Library of Trinity College, Dublin; and the National Library of Wales. These can be supplied by sending five copies for re-direction to:

MR A. T. SMAIL
Agent for Copyright Libraries,
100 Euston Street,
London
NW1 2HQ

Copyright

This is a complex and occasionally very technical area. There are books which explain the law more fully as it pertains to copyright in the UK and abroad (*see bibliography on p. 111*). Copyright exists in material which can be defined as intellectual property, that is, literary, dramatic, musical or artistic 'works', or any of the following 'subject matters': sound recordings, cinematograph films, television and sound broadcasts, cable programmes and published editions of works.

If a work was published in the UK during the author's lifetime, copyright, until 1995, subsisted in the work until 50 years from the end of the year of the author's death. In 1995 Britain came into line with European countries in copyright terms and it now extends to 70 years after the death of the author. This directive is intended to be applied retrospectively on works which have come into the public domain within the last twenty years. Regulations for the implementation of this directive are complex and expert advice should be sought by publishers who have titles on their lists which were previously out of copyright and which now fall within the 70-year rule.

The *Copyright, Designs and Patents Act 1988* has attempted to deal with the problem of ownership and copyright with regards to modern technology and associated new forms of storing, 'publishing' and retrieval of material. Again, the question of electronic rights remains complex and increasing use of the Internet makes defence of copyright, electronically, very complex.

Protection of copyright overseas remains a high priority for the British publishing industry. While 'piracy' of copyright works should decrease as more countries sign International Copyright Conventions, modern technology conspires to make such piracy temptingly easy. The moral rights of the author – the 'integrity' of the copyright holder – are also acknowledged by the Act. Further information may be obtained from:

THE BRITISH COPYRIGHT COUNCIL
29–33 Berners Street,
London W1P 4AA
Tel/fax: 0171 359 1895

Permissions for photocopying in academic and educational institutions are dealt with by:

THE COPYRIGHT LICENSING AGENCY LTD
90 Tottenham Court Road,
London
W1P 0LP
Tel: 0171 436 5931   **Fax**: 0171 436 3986
See also p. 68

See also p. 68

————————————Copyright permissions————————————

It is normally the author's or editor's responsibility to obtain (and pay for) permission to quote written material which is still in copyright. Permission should always be sought from the publisher of the quoted work, not the author. In complex cases, such as an anthology, however, the publisher often does this work for the author. Fees for quotation vary and there is no standard scale.

British copyright law allows free use of copyright material in two specific instances – when the material is used as part of a review or when used in research/private study.

Acknowledgements

The sources of all in-copyright quotations (words or music), tables and illustrations should be given, whether or not it was necessary to obtain permission for their use. In law 'sufficient acknowledgement' means at least the author (composer, artist and so on) and title.

The Net Book Agreement

The Net Book Agreement (NBA) was in existence in one form or another in Britain from 1900. It was set up as a publishers' agreement, under which rules were set out for the supply and sales of books through bookshops and other retailers. The latest agreement lasted from 1957, after its passage through the Restrictive Practices Court in 1962.

Under the terms of the agreement, publishers are free to decide if they wish to publish their books at net prices or not. Once they have decided to do so, the price cannot be reduced by a bookseller.

In late 1995, a number of large publishers decided to withdraw from the Agreement and publish their books non-net. This meant that discounted books could be sold by any bookshop who dealt in these titles. At the time of writing, the framework of the Net Book Agreement remains in force and publishers may still choose to publish within it, but the situation is constantly changing.

Grants to Publishers

In recognition of the pivotal position of publishing, extensive support is given to experienced publishers by the Scottish Arts Council in the form of grants towards the production costs of certain categories of books. The conditions and criteria attached to the 'Grants to Publishers' scheme and an application form are available on request. Submissions from publishers are considered four times a year by a special panel, which then makes recommendations to the Literature Committee.

The Council also recognises the importance of a vigorous publishing industry in Scotland by making an annual grant to the Scottish Publishers Association to promote co-operative ventures. As Gaelic publishing is a specialist matter the Council gives an annual grant to The Gaelic Books Council which then assists the writing, production, promotion and selling of books worthy of support. The Association for Scottish Literary Studies is also supported by the Scottish Arts Council.

Further information can be obtained from the Scottish Arts Council (*see p. 55*).

Publishing Training

THE PAUL HAMLYN FOUNDATION
Sussex House, 12 Upper Mall, London W6 9TA
Tel: 0181 741 2812
Fax: 0181 741 2263

The charitable foundation was set up in 1987 by Paul Hamlyn. It makes significant contributions to charitable causes in the Arts, education, book publishing and the Third World. The Foundation's support for book publishing concentrates on training and education. It is designed to encourage the raising of training standards in the UK and to make skills training available to those working in the industry who might not otherwise be offered training opportunities.

Training grants are available for employees, or regular freelancers, of small independent publishers; a bursary fund was given to London College of Printing and Distributive Trades, Thames Valley University and West Herts College to support students embarking on diploma/post-graduate courses in publishing. It is highly likely that the Foundation will re-launch its Skills Training Grants for Freelancers in Publishing in spring 1997.

New initiatives include: the Hamlyn Prize for the best student dissertation/project in under-graduate and postgraduate publishing study; support for the Federation of Children's Book Groups', Children's Book Awards; traineeships at AN Publications in Sunderland; and a Black Publishing Training Initiative in association with Yorkshire & Humberside Arts and Peepal Tree Press.

Further information about the Foundation is avaiable from Manick Govinda, Arts & Book Publishing Projects Officer, at the above address.

Other useful contact:
Book House Training Centre, *45 East Hill, Wandsworth, London SW18 2QZ. Tel: 0181 874 2718/4608. Fax: 0181 870 8985. E-mail: training@bhtc.eunet.co.uk*

GLASGOW COLLEGE OF BUILDING AND PRINTING

Faculty of Visual Communication, 60 North Hanover Street, Glasgow G1 2BP
Tel: 0141 332 9969
Fax: 0141 332 5170
The College's Faculty of Visual Communication offers a wide range of courses for those in the publishing industry. They are available at National Certificate, Higher National Certificate/Diploma through to Advanced Diploma level and many can be studied by full-time, day release or evening class. Courses include: Graphics; Art and Design; Photography; Printing; Fine Bookbinding and Book Repair; Graphic Reproduction; Electronic Publishing; Information and Media Technology; Multimedia Development and Production; Illustration; TV Production.

Further details on courses and how to apply can be obtained from the marketing section at the College.

NAPIER UNIVERSITY

Department of Print Media, Publishing and Communication, Craighouse Road, Edinburgh EH10 5LG
Tel: 0131 444 2266 Ext. 2569
Fax: 0131 452 8532
Full-time, four-year BA Honours degree in Publishing, building on strengths of Diploma in Publishing offered since 1968. Cognate courses include Journalism, Communication and Graphic Communications Management. The Department also offers customised in-service courses for publishing houses and related organisations from copy-editing to new production technology. The Department houses the Scottish Colour Centre and Centre for Publishing Development. Further information is available from the above address.

OPEN UNIVERSITY VALIDATION SERVICES (formerly Publishing Qualifications Board)

344–354 Gray's Inn Road, London WC1X 8BP
Tel: 0171 278 4411
Fax: 0171 833 1012
Contact: Rosie Thom
Services offered: National Vocational Qualifications for the publishing industry which include occupational specific qualifications and others which might be relevant, ie: Management Training and Development
Description of services: Administer National and Scottish Vocational Qualifications covering ten different industries including publishing.

ROBERT GORDON UNIVERSITY, THE

School of Information and Media, 352 King Street, Aberdeen AB24 5BN
Tel: 01224 262951
Fax: 01224 262969
E-mail: slis@rgu.ac.uk

Applicants who wish to enter the traditional publishing/bookselling sectors, the areas of the industry producing serials, magazines or the newer electronic media, may enter the full-time, three-year BA course, the four-year BA (Hons) course, or the one year postgraduate diploma and linked Masters degree programme. For staff already employed in the industry, a postgraduate certificate or diploma programme with a linked Masters (MA/MSc) degree is available by distance learning over one to three years. Areas of study include print technology, retailing, business studies, editorial studies, design, mass communication and electronic publishing. Further information from the secretary at the above address.

SCOTTISH PUBLISHERS ASSOCIATION

Scottish Book Centre, 137 Dundee Street, Edinburgh EH11 1BG
Tel: 0131 228 6866
Fax: 0131 228 3220

A comprehensive programme runs throughout the year covering a variety of topics ranging from fundamental skills to appraisals of current issues and trends within publishing. Courses are led by practitioners in each field and popular seminars provide the opportunity to meet informally with others in the book trade. The programme offers substantial savings on courses held outside Scotland. The courses are open to everyone, with SPA and SBMG members enjoying preferential rates. For further details or for the SPA course brochure, contact Allan Shanks at the above address.

UNIVERSITY OF STIRLING

The Centre for Publishing Studies, University of Stirling, Stirling FK9 4LA
Tel: 01786 473171
Fax: 01786 466210

One-year postgraduate MPhil course in Publishing Studies, giving an overview of industry structure, varieties of jobs, kinds of editing, production (including word-processing, desktop publishing, electronic and internet). Graduates have mainly found editorial and marketing jobs in Scotland and England; others are in production control, bookselling or related fields. Further information available from the above address.

See also Women in Publishing Scotland, p. 73 and the Society of Freelance Editors and Proofreaders, p. 72

BOOKSELLERS

SCOTTISH BOOK MARKETING GROUP

Scottish Book Centre, 137 Dundee Street, Edinburgh
EH11 1BG
Tel: 0131 228 6866
Scottish Book Marketing Group
Fax: 0131 228 3220
Date established: 1986
Contacts: Joanna Mattinson; Susanne Gilmour
Services offered: Scottish Book Fortnight; fortnightly, quarterly and annual Scottish Bestseller Lists; spring/summer promotion and guide; Scottish Book Marketing Group Contribution Award; BA *Books for Giving* Christmas catalogue, Scottish supplement; collaborative projects; information and advisory service; access to reference and resource material; purpose-built venue for meetings, training courses or conferences

The Scottish Book Marketing Group (SBMG) is a unique venture – indigenous to Scotland – set up by the Scottish Publishers Association and the Booksellers Association (Scottish Branch). Its aims are to promote Scottish books through Scottish bookshops, with the help of libraries and arts organisations, to create a wider public awareness of their quality, vibrant range and availability – as well as to provide a platform for Scottish writers. A wide readership is, therefore, encouraged to explore the Scottish section of a local bookshop and to discover new writing. Current SBMG membership consists of over 45 bookseller members, including independents, chains and wholesalers, who are listed on the following pages. Full membership and seasonal membership schemes are available to bookselling outlets.

To date, SBMG activities have been concerned with six major initiatives:

• A fortnightly Bestseller List for Scotland, reflecting cultural diversity and regional differences, which appears regularly in the press. A 'one-stop' review copy service is also offered to media contacts. A list highlighting bestsellers of the year in Scotland is also compiled and quarterly lists, covering various topics.

• A nationwide autumn promotion, Scottish Book Fortnight (SBF), which presents a showcase of selected new Scottish titles. Held annually in October, SBF promotes Scottish titles with a full free author events programme and displays throughout the country.

In 1996, the Readiscovery Book Bus formed part of the Authors on Tour programme. In total Scottish Book Fortnight 1996 involved over 40 authors in over 100 events at bookshops, libraries and schools. (Dates for the 1997 promotion are Saturday 18th October to Saturday 1st November.)

- A summer books promotion aimed at the large Scottish tourist and visitor markets. This promotion is centred on a free, colour brochure featuring both new and backlist titles, across a dynamic range of subjects.
- In 1994, the SBMG Contribution Award was introduced – an exciting annual trade presentation (*see p. 98 for further information*). This award aims to recognise the outstanding contribution made by an individual, body or group (working within the industry) to the Scottish book trade. Scottish booksellers, publishers and librarians submit nominations, create the shortleet and select the recipient. The SBMG Contribution Award 1996, sponsored by BPC Books and Information, was presented to James Thin Ltd, South Bridge Edinburgh branch. Previous Award winners include: John Lennie of Seol Ltd (1995); Tom Farries of T.C. Farries & Co (1994).
- An information and advisory service for all members. Staff and members are keen to develop and strengthen the activities' programme of the Group and to encourage new members. As the organisation is based in the Scottish Book Centre, all members have access to the fully equipped meeting room for conference and training purposes.
- A collaborative project to produce a Scottish supplement in the Booksellers Association *Books for Giving* Christmas catalogue. Introduced in 1995.

The SBMG receives support and sponsorship from the following: Bookspeed; BPC Books and Information (sponsors of the SBMG Contribution Award); Eden Court Theatre (Inverness); Invergordon Distillers/Whyte & Mackay Group; The National Trust for Scotland; Royal Lyceum Theatre (Edinburgh); ScotRail; *Scotland on Sunday*, *The Scotsman*; The Scottish Arts Council.

The SBMG is run by a committee comprising equally of bookseller and publisher members plus Scottish library and author representatives. The Group is administered by the Scottish Publishers Association and has the support of the Association's staff and services.

Scottish Book Marketing Group

Member Booksellers

BLACKWELL'S

12–14 Upperkirkgate, Aberdeen AB10 1BG
Tel: 01224 644528
Fax: 01224 630032
Contacts: Mrs Judi Whitefoot (Manager);
Mr Anthony F. Schmitz (Centre Manager)
Subject specialisations: HMSO database interrogation and ordering, bibliographic searching and supply

DILLONS BOOKSTORE

269–271 Union Street, Aberdeen AB11 6BR
Tel: 01224 210161
Fax: 01224 211808
Contact: Richard Hills (Manager)
Subject specialisations: Scottish, computing, children's

WATERSTONE'S BOOKSELLERS

236 Union Street, Aberdeen AB10 1TN
Tel: 01224 571655
Fax: 01224 213667
Contacts: John Green (Manager); Fiona Watson (Assistant Manager)

Aviemore

JAMES THIN LTD

87 Grampian Road, Aviemore PH22 1RH
Tel: 01479 810797
Contact: Ann Stewart (Manager)

Ayr

JAMES THIN LTD

15 Sandgate, Ayr KA7 1BG
Tel: 01292 611011
Fax: 01292 269298
Contacts: Phyllis Weir (Manager); Brenda Law (Assistant Manager)
Subject specialisations: Scottish and local interest

BOOKSELLERS

LANDMARK BOOKSHOP

Landmark Centre, Carr Bridge, Inverness-shire PH23 3AJ
Tel: 01479 841613
Fax: 01479 841384
Contacts: Mrs Una Leitch; Mrs Dorothy Wedderburn
Subject specialisations: Natural history; Scottish interest and history, children's; hobbies, walking

THE DORNOCH BOOKSHOP

High Street, Dornoch, Sutherland IV25 3SH
Tel: 01862 810165
Fax: 01862 810197
Contact: Richard Butterworth (Proprietor)
Subject specialisations: Scotland (the Highlands in particular), golf, children's books

THE BOOK PLACE

T. C. Farries & Co. (Library Supplier), Irongray Road, Lochside, Dumfries DG2 0LH
Tel: 01387 720755
Fax: 01387 721105
Contacts: Catherine Brickwood (Purchasing Manager); Robert Hawthorn (Retail Manager)

JAMES THIN LTD

18–26 Church Crescent, Dumfries DG1 1DQ
Tel: 01387 254288
Fax: 01387 257242
Contact: Lorraine McLean (Manager)

BROWSERS' BOOKSHOP

25 High Street, Dunblane, Perthshire FK15 0EE
Tel: 01786 824738
Contact: Louis Stott (Owner)
Subject specialisations: Scottish, children's books, general and literary fiction, folklore, poetry, France and French books

JAMES THIN LTD
7–8 High Street, Dundee DD1 1SS
Tel: 01382 223999
Fax: 01382 202963
Contact: Gordon Dow (Manager)
Subject specialisations: General, academic, local interest, Scottish titles

JOHN SMITH & SON (GLASGOW) LTD
Dundee University Bookshop, College Green, Dundee DD1 4HN
Tel: 01382 202790
Fax: 01382 204718
E-mail: dd@johnsmith.co.uk
Subject specialisations: Academic; civil/electronic/mechanical engineering; bio-sciences; dentistry; Scots & English law; American & European studies.

WATERSTONE'S BOOKSELLERS
35 Commercial Street, Dundee DD1 3DG
Tel: 01382 200322
Fax: 01382 201730
Contacts: Jane Diamond (Manager); Denise Dolan (Assistant Manager); Andrew Forrester (Assistant Manager)
Subject specialisations: Fiction, Scottish fiction, Scottish travel, Science Fiction, Scottish law, children's books, general fiction

LAING'S BOOKSHOP
10 Maygate, Dunfermline KY12 7NH
Tel/fax: 01383 733239
Contact: Alan Laing (Manager)

BOOKPOINT
147–149 Argyll Street, Dunoon PA23 7DD
Tel/fax: 01369 702377
Contact: Fiona Roy (Manager)
Subject specialisations: Wide selection of Scottish books – fiction and non-fiction

BOOKSELLERS

BOOKSPEED (wholesaler)

62 Hamilton Place, Edinburgh EH3 5AZ
Tel: 0131 225 4950
Fax: 0131 220 6515
Contacts: Kingsley Dawson (Director); Annie Rhodes (Director)
Subject specialisations: Scottish, travel guides and maps, general and mass-market, reference, gift books, children's. Subsidies and advice on shelving.

JAMES THIN LTD

57 George Street, Edinburgh EH2 2JQ
Tel: 0131 225 4495
Fax: 0131 225 9626
Contacts: Robb Stainsby (Manager); Andrew Smith (Assistant Manager); Lorna Dixon (Events)
Subject specialisations: Fiction, reference, maps, travel, business, cookery, children's

JAMES THIN LTD

Gyle Shopping Centre, South Gyle Broadway, Edinburgh EH12 9JT
Tel: 0131 539 7757
Fax: 0131 538 7758
Contacts: Susan Martin (Manager); Billy Nisbet (Assistant Manager)
Subject specialisations: General bookshop with strong children's department

JAMES THIN LTD

Winner of 1996 SBMG Contribution Award

53–59 South Bridge, Edinburgh EH1 1YS
Tel: 0131 556 6743
Fax: 0131 557 8149
Contacts: Ainslie Thin (Chairman); James Shaw (Bookshop Manager); Patricia Britton (Events and Marketing)
Subject specialisations: General and academic books, also antiquarian and second-hand

JAMES THIN LTD

Waverley Shopping Centre, Edinburgh EH1 1BQ
Tel/fax: 0131 557 1378
Contact: Maggie Rodan (Manager)

KAY'S BOOKSHOP

390 Morningside Road, Edinburgh EH10 5HX
Tel: 0131 447 1265
Contact: Ian Taylor (Proprietor)

WATERSTONE'S BOOKSELLERS
83 George Street, Edinburgh EH2 3ES
Tel: 0131 225 3436
Fax: 0131 226 4548
Contacts: Allan Watson
Subject specialisations: Children's books, fiction, Scottish fiction, fine art, biography

WATERSTONE'S BOOKSELLERS
East End Branch, 13–14 Princes Street, Edinburgh EH2 2AN
Tel: 0131 556 3034
Fax: 0131 557 8801
Contacts: Iain MacFarlane (Manager); Patrick Booth (Deputy Manager); Bob McDevitt (Marketing); Karin Anderson (Institutional sales)
Subject specialisations: Scottish interest, fiction, computing, children's, cookery, travel, sport and gender issues

WATERSTONE'S BOOKSELLERS
West End Branch, 128 Princes Street, Edinburgh EH2 4AD
Tel: 0131 226 2666
Fax: 0131 226 4689
Contacts: Matthew Perren (Manager); Sarah Woodcock (Events)
Subject specialisations: Scottish, academic, reference, language

————————— Fraserburgh —————————

JOHN TRAIL LTD
9 Mid Street, Fraserburgh AB43 9AJ
Tel/fax: 01346 513307
Contact: Mrs May Maitland (Proprietor)
Subject specialisations: Scottish, local interest, children's, general fiction, reference

————————— Glasgow —————————

DILLONS BOOKSTORE
174–176 Argyle Street, Glasgow G2 8AH
Tel: 0141 248 4814
Fax: 0141 248 4622
E-mail: glasgow@dillons.eunet.co.uk
Contacts: James Imrie (Manager); Graham Wilson
Subject specialisations: Scottish, cookery, computing, teaching, history, psychology, sociology, Science Fiction, medical

JOHN SMITH & SON (GLASGOW) LTD

252 Byres Road, Glasgow G12 8SH
Tel: 0141 334 2769
Fax: 0141 339 3744
E-mail: br@johnsmith.co.uk
Contact: Alison Stroak (Manager)
Subject specialisations: Three floors of bookselling specialising in paperback fiction, children's and music

JOHN SMITH & SON BOOKSHOPS

57 St Vincent Street, Glasgow G2 5TB
Tel: 0141 221 7472
Fax: 0141 248 4412
E-mail: 57@johnsmith.co.uk.
Contacts: Willie Anderson (Managing Director); Joan Douglas (General Manager)
Subject specialisations: Six floors of bookselling, covering all subjects, specialising in Scottish, fiction, children's, art, military history, travel guides, languages, foreign newspapers, management, law, sciences, computer books, teachers' resources, social sciences. Official stockist for HMSO and HSE publications. West of Scotland agent for Ordnance Survey maps. Extensive multimedia department with full demonstration hardware facilities.
Services include: Book ordering for any title not in stock; over two million titles on database; Booksearch service for out-of-print titles; access to French, German, Spanish, Italian and American Books in Print. Will send books to anywhere in the world.

MILNGAVIE BOOKSHOP

37 Douglas Street, Milngavie, Glasgow G62 6PE
Tel: 0141 956 4752
Fax: 0141 956 4819
Contact: Robin Lane (Partner)
Subject specialisations: Computing, multimedia, school textbooks, mail order, customer special orders, book tokens, stationery, greetings cards, videos

PICKERING & INGLIS

26 Bothwell Street, Glasgow G2 6PA
Tel: 0141 221 8913
Fax: 0141 204 1285
Contact: Nicholas Gray (Director)
Subject specialisations: Scottish, children's, Christian books and bibles

WATERSTONE'S BOOKSELLERS

45–50 Princes Square, Glasgow G1 3JN
Tel: 0141 221 9650
Fax: 0141 221 4971
Contacts: Robert Kinnear (Manager); Belinda MacDougall (Events)
Subject specialisations: Scottish fiction, history, art, travel,
biography, cookery, children's

WATERSTONE'S BOOKSELLERS

132 Union Street, Glasgow G1 3QQ
Tel: 0141 221 0890
Fax: 0141 221 4067
Contacts: Duncan Furness (Manager)
Subject specialisations: Scottish history, fiction, art

──────────── Greenock ────────────

BOOKPOINT

93 West Blackhall Street, Inverclyde PA15 1XP
Tel/fax: 01475 785050
Contact: Catherine Turnbull (Manager)

──────────── Helensburgh ────────────

BOOKWORMS

7 East Clyde Street, Helensburgh G84 7NY
Tel: 01436 674743
Fax: 01436 679954
Contacts: Ros Lane; Robin Lane
Subject specialisations: Multimedia, Scottish interest, mail order,
USA importing, special orders, Book Tokens, greetings cards

──────────── Inverness ────────────

JAMES THIN LTD

Melven's Bookshop, 29 Union Street, Inverness IV1 1QA
Tel: 01463 233500
Fax: 01463 711474
Contact: Mr Malcolm S. Herron (Manager); Mrs Doreen Herron
(Assistant Manager)
Subject specialisations: Scottish, hardback and paperback fiction
and non-fiction, extensive general stocks, audio books, computing,
business, CD-ROMs, children's educational texts, bargains, videos,
stationery, maps (local, foreign and large-scale mapping service
available), globes. Mail order service available.

C. & E. ROY
The Celtic House, Bowmore, Isle of Islay, Argyll PA43 7LD
Tel/fax: 01496 810304
Contact: Colin P. Roy (Manager)
Subject specialisations: Celtic, Scottish and local interest

RODERICK SMITH LTD
52 Point Street, Stornoway, Isle of Lewis HS1 2XF
Tel: 01851 702082
Fax: 01851 706644
Contact: Mrs Irene Matheson (Managing Director)
Subject specialisations: Local, Scottish, Gaelic, children's, general paperbacks

THE BOOK HOUSE
21–25 Tolbooth Street, Kirkcaldy, Fife KY1 1RW
Tel: 01592 265378
Fax: 01592 591300
Contact: Morag Robertson (Manager)
Subject specialisations: Computing, Scottish and local interest

JAMES THIN LTD
176 High Street, Perth PH1 5UN
Tel: 01738 35222
Fax: 01738 35223
Contacts: Sheila Lindsay (Book Manager, Events); Miss Marion McGregor (Shop Manager)

WATERSTONE'S BOOKSELLERS
St John's Centre, Perth PH1 5UX
Tel: 01738 630013
Fax: 01738 643478
Contact: Louise Cassells (Manager)
Subject specialisations: Scottish travel, Scottish fiction, Scottish biography, children's

J. & G. INNES LTD
107 South Street, St Andrews, Fife KY16 9QW
Tel: 01334 472174
Contact: Mrs P. M. Innes (Manager)
Subject specialisations: Scottish and local interest, general, children's

JOHN SMITH & SON (GLASGOW) LTD
127 Market Street, St Andrews, Fife KY16 9PE
Tel: 01334 475122
Fax: 01334 478035
E-mail: an@johnsmith.co.uk
Contact: Ken MacKenzie (Manager)
Subject specialisations: Paperbacks, maps, Scottish and local publications (computer link to Glasgow)

DILLONS BOOKSTORE
20–22 Murray Place, Stirling FK8 2DD
Tel: 01786 451141
Fax: 01786 474022
E-mail: stirling@dillons.euent.co.uk
Contact: Helen Donald
Subject specialisations: Scottish, general stockist

JOHN SMITH & SON (GLASGOW) LTD
The MacRobert Centre, University of Stirling, Stirling FK9 4LF
Tel: 01786 473891
Fax: 01786 447696
E-mail: bookshop@stirling.ac.uk
Contact: John Gray (Manager)
Subject specialisations: Academic textbooks, general, children's and stationery

ANN R. THOMAS GALLERY
Harbour Street, Tarbert, Argyll PA29 6UD
Tel/fax: 01880 820 390
Contact: Ann Thomas (Proprietor)
Subject specialisations: Nautical books and charts, Scottish interest, cookery, gardening, children's

BOOKSELLERS

THE CEILIDH PLACE BOOKSHOP

14 West Argyle Street, Ullapool, Ross and Cromarty IV26 2TY
Tel: 01854 612103
Fax: 01854 612886
Contact: Avril Moyes (Manager)
Subject specialisations: Literature and English literature; poetry; politics; art, music; history and natural history.

ORGANISATIONS

SCOTTISH ARTS COUNCIL

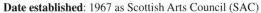

12 Manor Place, Edinburgh EH3 7DD
Tel: 0131 226 6051
Fax: 0131 225 9833
Date established: 1967 as Scottish Arts Council (SAC)
Contacts: Seona Reid (Director); Christine Hamilton (Director of Planning and Development); Graham Berry (Director of Finance & Administration); Andrew Nairne (Visual Arts Director); John Murphy (Combined Arts Director); Helen Bennett (Crafts Director); David Taylor (Drama and Dance Director); Jenny Brown (Literature Director); David Bonnar (Lottery Director); Matthew Rooke (Music Director)
Office hours: Mon–Thurs 9.00am–5.30pm; Fri 9.00am–5.00pm

Objectives

To develop and improve knowledge, understanding and practice of the arts and to increase their accessibility to the public throughout Scotland. A recent policy statement identified the Council's main aim as being to 'create a climate in which arts of quality flourish and are enjoyed by a wide range of people throughout Scotland'.

Activities

The Council itself does not administer orchestras, theatres, arts centres or festivals but grant-aids others to do so. Its officers act as assessors on boards of management of many of these organisations, which range in scale from local festivals and community arts groups, to major institutions, such as orchestras, opera and ballet companies, regional theatres and major arts centres. Many of these, for example, the opera, ballet, orchestras and some drama companies, tour widely throughout Scotland. In addition, the Council subsidises umbrella organisations such as Enterprise Music Scotland and the National Federation of Music Societies, which support the work of music clubs, arts guilds and amateur choirs and orchestras throughout Scotland.

The Council also operates schemes for awards, bursaries, fellowships and travel and research grants to writers, artists, composers, dancers, actors, playwrights and choreographers. A Council of fourteen meets six times a year to formulate and oversee the policies of the Scottish Arts Council (SAC). It is advised by a number of specialist artform committees and panels which are made up of people from all over Scotland who have expert knowledge of the arts and related interests.

Information

SAC offers a general advisory service on most aspects of the arts and publishes a number of reports, guides and bulletins about its work and the arts in Scotland in general. A list of publications is available from the Communications Department.

Literary magazines

A number of literary magazines are published with subsidy from SAC. These magazines may be obtained direct from the publishers or from bookshops. Some of the publications on pp. 102–106 receive subsidies from SAC.

BOOK TRUST SCOTLAND

Scottish Book Centre, 137 Dundee Street, Edinburgh
EH11 1BG
Tel: 0131 229 3663
Fax: 0131 228 4293
Contacts: Lindsey Fraser; Kathryn Ross; Chris Young

Book Trust Scotland – an independent, educational charity supported by the Scottish Arts Council – works throughout the country to promote books and the pleasures of reading to people of all ages. In order to disseminate information about books and reading, a range of agencies are used; for example *Radical Reading,* the campaign to encourage teenagers to pick up a book, utilised the skills of school and youth librarians, *Now Read On,* a public library based initiative for adult readers, has now expanded to include secondary schools and producing materials for *National Poetry Day*, involves a wide network of literary organisations, writers, writers' groups, venues and interested individuals.

A book information service answers queries from around the country on all aspects of the literary world. Information is held on most writers living in Scotland and there is an extensive collection of press cuttings on Scottish literary themes and issues.

A significant proportion of Book Trust Scotland's activities take place in the field of children's literature. Book Trust Scotland's reference library contains a copy of every book published in the UK for children within the last twelve months. It is a free resource for anyone with an interest in children's books and to make this excellent resource more widely available a newsletter, *Shelf life,* was launched in January 1996. *Shelf life* is a thrice yearly publication available to every school and public library in Scotland and includes reviews, recommendations, author profiles and book news with a particular commitment to Scottish writers, illustrators and publishers.

Book Trust Scotland produces and sells literary guides, poetry posters, children's book posters, and a variety of publications including a new edition of the popular – and essential – *Off the Shelf: A Guide to Scotland's Writers and Illustrators for Children* and *reading Glasgow: a literary guide to writers and books associated with the city* by Moira Burgess. Book Trust Scotland administers The McVitie's Prize for the Scottish Writer of the Year and The Fidler Award, an annual award for a first novel for children aged between 8 and 12 years (*see 'Prizes and Awards' section on pp. 95–99 for further information*).

READISCOVERY TOURING

Scottish Book Centre, 137 Dundee Street, Edinburgh
EH11 1BG
Tel: 0131 221 1995
Fax: 0131 228 4293
Contact: Janet Smyth (Project Coordinator)

Readiscovery
a Book Trust Scotland Project

Readiscovery Touring is the legacy of the Readiscovery Campaign and has become a Book Trust Scotland project dealing specifically with the Book Bus and the Scottish Touring Coordination Service.

The Book Bus continues its commitment to primary schools in far-flung areas, taking books and authors to these remote communities, far from a bookshop or library. During 1996 the bus visited, amongst other places, the Highlands, Orkney, Shetland and the Western Isles. Working closely with the resources available through the merge with Book Trust Scotland, Readiscovery has been able to expand the remit to include secondary schools, community festivals and partnerships with other literacy projects such as the Scottish Dyslexia Association.

The Scottish Touring Coordination Service produces a quarterly publication which aims to detail all literary events happening in Scotland within the 3 months covered. Included are literature festivals and exhibitions, news of planned author tours, and details of publishers' latest titles. The aim is to provide a comprehensive overview of literary activity taking place in the country. The service also provides a 'helpdesk' giving advice to promoters, authors, press etc.

It is through the Touring Coordination Service that Readiscovery and Book Trust Scotland are involved in National Poetry Day; together coordinating the production and distribution of the poetry postcards, posters and events brochure.

By the beginning of 1997, Readiscovery will have produced an update to *High Roads and Low Roads*, a guide for promoters organising author tours.

EDINBURGH BOOK FESTIVAL

Scottish Book Centre, 137 Dundee Street,
Edinburgh EH11 1BG
Tel: 0131 228 5444
Fax: 0131 228 4333
E-mail: admin@edbookfest.co.uk
Company established: 1982 (Edinburgh Book Fair Ltd)
Contacts: Jan Fairley (Director); Alison Plackitt (Assistant Director)
Date of next Book Festival: 9th–25th August 1997

The Edinburgh Book Festival (EBF) began in 1983 to promote and celebrate the written word. It throws the spotlight on national and international literature at a time when Edinburgh becomes a 'Festival City', one of the key cultural capitals of the world. In 1995, 79,000 visitors came to the Edinburgh Book Festival. EBF is one of the world's largest and liveliest book events attracting everyone from those who are mad about books to those who are more diffident, but who nonetheless cannot resist the attractions of its unique site in Charlotte Square in the heart of Edinburgh's Georgian city centre. In its desire to heighten public awareness of books and writing, as well as creating an inviting programme for adults, EBF aims to encourage young readers: many children come in family groups or with their school. In 1995, 36% of visitors came on their own and 44% in family groups.

EBF is a world of its own, housed in a series of marquees within Charlotte Square Gardens. The site comprises: two main book tents, where publishers display and sell their full range of titles and where readers browse (over £170,000 of books were sold in 1995); a Childrens's Book Tent with adjoining Children's Activity Tent; two theatres where the popular 'Meet the Author' events, readings, performances and lectures take place. It is hoped to increase the number of 'demonstration' events in 1997. EBF also has an irresistable central bar/cafe with an all-day cabaret stage. The site is arranged as a double courtyard, allowing visitors to sit, eat, drink, listen to musicians, read on the grass, or simply relax and talk to friends old and new.

EBF is distinguished by an extensive programme of readings, discussions, interviews, demonstrations, and performances. The Festival brings together new and established writers from home and abroad. Writers who appeared at EBF in 1995 included Yehuda Amichai, Iain Banks, Louis de Bernieres, Margaret Forster, Garrison Keillor, A.L. Kennedy, Doris Lessing, Eric Lomax, Terry Pratchett, Gitta Sereny, Colm Toibin, Rose Tremain,

Marina Warner, Mary Wesley. In 1997 on 9th/10th August, EBF will host the public literary events of the 64th International PEN Congress, organised by Scottish Pen, its main themes being identity and diversity, women and contemporary writing.

EBF's Children's Fair organises stimulating family and school events embracing story-tellings, workshops, readings and talks by authors and illustrators. In this way children have their first memorable experiences of meeting their favourite writers face-to-face. In 1995 writers included Anne Fine, Debi Gliori, Mairi Hedderwick, Shirley Hughes, Aileen Paterson, Michael Rosen, Roger McGough.

Since 1983 EBF has been a biennial event but it is hoped to move towards becoming an annual event by holding Festivals in both 1997 and 1998. In September 1996 EBF created a new core logo – an animated book – to achieve continuity of image and instant recognition.

In November 1996 EBF organised a very succesful 11 day series of 'Meet the Author' events at the Traverse Theatre, Edinburgh, called 'Writing November'. This included a number of innovative family events bringing together readings with slides, music, animated film and poetry.

GAELIC BOOKS COUNCIL, THE

22 Mansfield Street, Glasgow G11 5QP
Tel: 0141 337 6211
Contact: Ian MacDonald

The Council was set up in 1968 at the University of Glasgow but is now a separate organisation in its own right. Its purpose is to assist and stimulate Gaelic publishing. It has eight members drawn from various relevant areas of interest, one assessor from the Scottish Arts Council and a paid staff that has varied between two and three. The Scottish Arts Council has been its main funding body since 1983.

The Council itself provides financial assistance in the form of publication grants (paid to the publisher) for individual Gaelic books submitted by the publisher just before publication. The Council also operates a scheme of commission grants for books as yet unwritten. In the case of the commission grants, the author or publisher can approach the Council with a project, or vice-versa.

As a book retailer, the Council provides a postal service in the UK and beyond, as well as mounting one-off sales at special events such as Mods, weekend courses, conferences and other gatherings. It stocks all Gaelic and Gaelic-related books in print, and these are listed in its catalogue *Leabhraichean Gàidhlig*, first published in 1975 and subsequently updated at intervals. Two issues of a book news magazine, *Facal air an Fhacal*, were produced in the 1980s, and it is hoped to resume publication of this as pressure of work allows.

An editorial service is also available, and the Council regularly word-processes and prepares texts for the press. More details of its work may be obtained from its Annual Reports, which are available to the public free.

SCOTTISH BOOK CENTRE
137 Dundee Street Edinburgh EH11 1BG

The proposal for a Scottish Book Centre in Edinburgh, to meet the needs of the growing publishing industry and the development of literary promotions in Scotland, was first put forward in 1988. It was perhaps the largest single initiative for books in Scotland for several decades and a major move to restore Edinburgh to its former position of eminence within the publishing scene. The premises at Fountainbridge Library had been used for storage for some 20 years and the task of renovation was enormous. Offices for the Scottish Publishers Association, the Edinburgh Book Festival and Book Trust Scotland were created, together with conference and display facilities, space for meetings and book launches, for training courses and press briefings.

The Scottish Book Centre is a centre for professional publishing training; it holds programmes of author events; has display facilities which are open to teachers, librarians, writers and booksellers as well as to publishers, and the facilities are offered to other book-related organisations.

Setting up the project took a great deal of money and many funding bodies and sponsors made it possible – a full list is on display in the Scottish Book Centre. To them we owe many thanks. We hope that all sections of the book world in Scotland will continue to make full use of this resource.

T. C. Farries Room

The T. C. Farries Room is a self-contained suite within the Scottish Book Centre, with kitchen and cloakroom facilities, which seats around 40 people in rows or 20–25 around tables. It is available for meetings, conferences, book launches, prize awards and exhibitions. The room is available for hire at a moderate charge to outside organisations whilst SPA member publishers may have some free use of the room each year.

For booking details please contact the SPA on 0131 228 6866.

The room was provided for the Scottish Book Centre by T. C. Farries & Co Ltd, a major Scottish-based supplier to libraries in Scotland, the UK and world-wide (*see p. 89 for further information*).

SCOTTISH BOOK SOURCE

137 Dundee Street Edinburgh EH11 1BG
Tel: 0131 229 6800
Fax: 0131 229 9070
Established: 1995
Contacts: Lavinia Drew (Manager); Christine McPhillips,
Alison Rae, Andrew McDougall (Customer Service);
David Warnock (Warehouse Manager)
Directors: Christian Maclean, Michael Miller, Keith Whittles,
Lorraine Fannin

Scottish Book Source (SBS) was set up in 1995 to offer
distribution services to Scottish publishers. Initially the service
worked in collaboration with Albany Publishers' Distribution
which was under administrative pressure. When Albany
Publishers' Distribution ceased trading in early 1996, Scottish
Book Source took over the full warehousing, distribution,
invoicing and credit control function.

The warehouse for SBS is in Glasgow at 32 Finlas Street,
Springburn, managed by David Warnock who has had almost a
decade of book distribution experience. The administration,
customer and information service is based at the Scottish Book
Centre under the management of Lavinia Drew. SBS is owned
by the Scottish Publishers Association (which is the majority
shareholder) and a number of individual publishers.

At the end of the first year of operation, Scottish Book Source
is distributing books worldwide with 22 client publishers using
the service.

SCOTTISH LIBRARY ASSOCIATION

Scottish Centre for Information and Library Services,
1 John Street, Hamilton ML3 7EU
Tel: 01698 458888
Fax: 01698 458899
Company established: 1908
Contact: Robert Craig BA, MA, ALA (Director)
Services offered: Promotion of libraries and librarianship

What is the Association?

The Scottish Library Association was founded in 1908 as an independent association. In 1931 it entered into union with the Library Association in Scotland. The Library Association, the professional body for librarians and information specialists in the United Kingdom, was founded in 1877 and received a Royal Charter in 1898. It is a registered charity.

From only 65 members in 1908, the Scottish Library Association now has over 2,300, covering all aspects of library and information work. The expansion mirrors the development of library and information services and their increasing importance in many aspects of Scottish life.

What does it do?

The Association's main aims are the promotion of libraries and librarianship, the improvement of library services and the qualifications and status of librarians.

It pursues these aims by:

• Producing and promoting standards for library and information services.
• Presenting the views of members to central and local government, to the Convention of Scottish Local Authorities (COSLA), Royal Commissions, Committees of Inquiry and other bodies on a wide range of topics.
• Negotiating and consulting with other national bodies involved in the cultural and educational life of Scotland.
• Organising a wide range of meetings, conferences and weekend schools to keep members informed of developments in librarianship.
• Advising members on careers, offering guidance on salary levels and co-operating with trade unions to improve salaries and conditions of service.

The Association ensures that the voice of the profession is heard on matters of major significance which affect library services.

Publications

The Association publishes a wide range of material including an annual survey of public library expenditure, the directory, *Library and Information Resources*, and a directory of Scottish local studies information. Six times a year it issues a magazine, *Scottish Libraries*, to enable members to keep abreast of new developments in the profession. The Association also publishes material of Scottish local and national interest.

How is it funded?

The Scottish Library Association derives its funding from members' subscriptions and from income generated from the sale of publications, conferences and short courses.

The way ahead

• Supporting the Scottish Library and Information Council.
• Improving the coordination of library and information services.
• Strengthening the role of library services in the community.

ORGANISATIONS

SCOTTISH POETRY LIBRARY

Tweeddale Court, 14 High Street, Edinburgh EH1 1TE
Tel: 0131 557 2876
Association established: 1982; Limited company
formed 1994
Contacts: Tessa Ransford (Director); Penny Duce (Librarian)
Services offered: Borrowing and reference library; research
assistance and information; travelling van service to schools, prisons,
community centres
Description of services: The Scottish Poetry Library (SPL), a
registered charity open since February 1984, aims to make the poetry
of Scotland, in whatever language and a selection of mainly modern
poetry from other countries, visible and freely accessible to the
general public throughout the country. The resources and services
provided include the following:

- 20th century Scottish poetry and an interesting selection of modern poetry from all over the world are available in the library, with older poetry also well represented.
- Borrowing is free, apart from a charge of £0.50 per item borrowed by post. Freepost return labels are provided.
- The SPL has a reference collection of around 14,000 items and lending stock of around 8,000 volumes. Printed catalogues of the lending collection have been published in 1988 and 1991 (price £5.00 for the two including postage); another supplement will update this in due course.
- The SPL has pioneered a computerised index to poetry called INSPIRE: **IN**ternational and **S**cottish **P**oetry **I**nformation **RE**source. This allows people to search for poetry under their own terms, controlled by a comprehensive thesaurus of subjects. Twenty Scottish literary magazines published over the past 40 years have also been indexed and are being published (*The Scottish Poetry Index*).
- Current editions of literary magazines are on sale in the Library and back numbers may be consulted.
- Audio and video tapes for borrowing and consulting are also provided. The stock of these is steadily increasing.
- The SPL Newsletter keeps the membership, currently over 750 individuals and organisations, in touch. The annual subscription is £10.00 for individuals and £15.00 for organisations.

ASSOCIATION OF AUTHORS' AGENTS

c/o Greene and Heaton Ltd, 37 Goldhawk Road, London W12 8QQ
Tel: 0181 749 0315
Fax: 0181 749 0318
Contact: Carol Heaton (Secretary)
Objectives: To institute and maintain a code of professional practice to which all members of the Association shall commit themselves and to discuss matters of common professional interest. Membership is only open to literary agents who have been in business for a minimum of three years.

AUTHOR–PUBLISHER NETWORK

6 Kelvinbrook, West Molesey, Surrey KT8 1RZ
Tel/fax: 0181 979 3060
E-mail: 1101655.3235@compuserve.com
Contact: Daphne Macara (Secretary)
Objectives: To advise and assist writers, illustrators and poets to produce their self-published books, booklets and manuals and newsletters to professional standards. Membership is open to all who want to take control of their own work. Subscription: 1996–97 £15.00 p.a.
Description of services: Author–Publisher Network (A–PN) publishes a twice yearly *Catalogue of Members Books*, an annual *Directory of Members* and regular *Reviews Supplements of Members' Books*. A–PN's bi-monthly news-journal, *Write to PUBLISH*, contains information on new technology, book production and marketing. *SMALL PUBLISHERS A–Z: The Guide to Good Publishing*, price £5.00 post free, is to be published autumn 1996.

BOOK MARKETING LIMITED (BML)

7a Bedford Square, London WC1B 3RA
Tel: 0171 580 7282
Fax: 0171 580 7236
Contact: Steven Bohme
Objectives: To provide an information and research service of the highest standard to companies within, or interested in, the book trade.
Description of services: BML maintains a library of information about the book trade; carries out *ad hoc* surveys of the trade and consumers; runs *Books and the Consumer* – the definitive, continuous survey of book-buying and reading habits in Britain; and publishes various reports on the book industry.

BOOKSELLERS ASSOCIATION: SCOTTISH BRANCH

Honorary Secretary, c/o Milngavie Bookshop, 37 Douglas Street, Milngavie, Glasgow G62 6PE

Tel: 0141 956 4752

Fax: 0141 956 4819

Contacts: Patricia Britton (Chairman); Robin Lane (Honorary Secretary)

Objectives: The Association promotes and protects the interests of booksellers in Scotland and the UK.

Description of services: Branch activities serve as a forum for the exchange of views between booksellers and promotes sales of Scottish books, Scottish authors, Book Token sales, booksellers' clearing house and Scottish Book Marketing Group participation, maintaining close links with the Scottish Publishers Association.

BRITISH COUNCIL, THE

Information Services Management, Medlock Street, Manchester M15 4AA

Tel: 0161 957 7178

Fax: 0161 957 7168

Contacts: Head/Book and Media Promotion Unit

Objectives: To promote Britain and British ideas by helping to make British books available overseas, working closely with the UK book trade

Description of services: 1. Provide high-quality presence at a selection of international book fairs and exhibitions. 2. To provide information on overseas book markets to UK publishers and booksellers. 3. To support the development of commercial links between overseas and UK book industries through training, consultancy and attachments.

COPYRIGHT LICENSING AGENCY LTD, THE

90 Tottenham Court Road, London W1P 0LP

Tel: 0171 436 5931

Fax: 0171 436 3986

Contact: Colin P. Hadley (Chief Executive & Company Secretary)

Objectives: The Agency was formed in 1882 by the Authors' Licensing & Collecting Society and the Publishers Licensing Society as a single source for the authorisation of copying and to establish and manage licensing schemes for institutional and professional organisations where extensive photocopying of books, journals and periodicals occurs.

Description of services: The issuing and administration of copying licenses and the distribution of the copying fees (via their respective societies) to those British and foreign authors and publishers whose works have been copied.

FEDERATION OF CHILDREN'S BOOK GROUPS

c/o Alison Dick, 6 Bryce Place, Currie, Midlothian EH14 5LR

Objectives: A voluntary organisation for parents, teachers, librarians, booksellers, publishers and all who are interested in books and children from 0 to 16 years.

Description of services: Local groups fit local circumstances: activities range from talks, books sales, Family Reading Groups and story times to sponsored author visits and out-of-school fun events. National events include National Tell a Story Week and annual conferences. Booklists are published regularly and include *Pick of the Year* – 50 top titles tested and chosen by children and families for the Children's Book Award.

INTERNATIONAL BOOK DEVELOPMENT LTD

500 Chiswick High Road, London W4 5RG

Tel: 0181 742 7474

Fax: 0181 747 8715

Contacts: Tony Read; David Foster; Amanda Buchan; Carmelle Denning; Euan Henderson

Objectives: To work for the comprehensive development of book provision and book markets world-wide; to encourage investment in books and journals world-wide by governments, aid organisations and book trade bodies, backed by careful planning and implementation.

Description of services: 1. Provision of expert consultancy services world-wide to aid organisations, governments and book trade bodies. 2. Information and advisory services to publishers, booksellers and others on subscription. 3. Training services to aid-funded projects overseas. 4. Administration of the British government's subsidised book schemes for developing countries (ELBS) and for central and eastern Europe (LPBB).

POETRY ASSOCIATION OF SCOTLAND

The Orchard, Muirton, Auchterarder, Perthshire PH3 1ND

Tel: 01764 662211

Contact: Robin Bell (General Secretary)

Objectives: A registered charity promoting poetry through readings and related activities.

Description of services: The Association was founded in 1924 and is dedicated to promoting poetry in all the languages of Scotland and to staging readings by major poets from all over the UK and overseas. Most performance events are staged at the Netherbow Theatre in Edinburgh and lectures are given at the School of Scottish Studies, Edinburgh University.

SCOTTISH ASSOCIATION OF PUBLISHERS' EDUCATIONAL REPRESENTATIVES (SAPER)

c/o 24 Redmill Cottages, East Whitburn, West Lothian EH47 0JR
Tel: 01501 741807
Contact: Janis Stewart (Honorary Secretary)
Objectives: To give expression to opinion of members and to encourage a professional approach to the promotion of texts and materials in educational establishments throughout Scotland
Description of services: SAPER provides a regular circular of information and requests for display materials to educational representatives of nearly all major publishers: items for inclusion can be sent to the Honorary Secretary (at the above address) from whom details of SAPER's regular diet of Scottish educational exhibitions are also available.

SCOTTISH BRAILLE PRESS

Craigmillar Park, Edinburgh EH16 5NB
Tel: 0131 662 4445
Fax: 0131 662 1968
Contact: Mr J. H. Adams
Description of services: Since its establishment in 1891, the Scottish Braille Press has grown to become one of the world's leading producers of reading material for blind people. As well as printing material for other organisations including RNIB, UNESCO and the BBC, the Scottish Braille Press also publishes, *The Braille Sporting Record, Madam, Home Help, Spectrum, Tempo, Braille Science Journal*. The Scottish Braille Press also produces braille editions of print bestsellers, tactile diagrams, exam papers and information manuals.

SCOTTISH NEWSPAPER PUBLISHERS ASSOCIATION

48 Palmerston Place, Edinburgh EH12 5DE
Tel: 0131 220 4353
Fax: 0131 220 4344
Contact: J. B. Raeburn (Director)
Objectives: To promote and represent the interests of the Scottish weekly newspaper industry
Description of services: The Association is the employers' organisation/trade association for the weekly newspaper industry in Scotland. Its principal areas of activity embrace industrial relations, education and training, newsprint, self-regulation and lobbying on issues of direct concern to the industry.

SCOTTISH PRINT EMPLOYERS FEDERATION

48 Palmerston Place, Edinburgh EH12 5DE
Tel: 0131 220 4353
Fax: 0131 220 4344
Contact: J. B. Raeburn (Director)
Objectives: To promote and represent the interests of the Scottish printing industry
Description of services: The Federation is the employers' organisation/trade association for all sectors of the printing industry in Scotland. Its principal services embrace industrial relations, education and training, health and safety, productivity and profitability and wages surveys, commercial matters and lobbying on issues of direct concern to the industry.

SCOTTISH PRINTING ARCHIVAL TRUST

5 Abercorn Avenue, Edinburgh EH8 7HP
Tel: 0131 661 3791
Contact: Mr J. C. Keppie (Honorary Secretary)
Objectives: To record information, institute research and acquire material relating to the development of Scottish printing for the benefit of the public and print media education
Description of services: Advisory, informatory and facilitatory

SOCIETY OF AUTHORS IN SCOTLAND, THE

24 March Hall Crescent, Edinburgh EH16 5HL
Tel: 0131 667 5230
Contact: Alanna Knight (Secretary)
Objectives: Founded with the object of representing, assisting and protecting writers.
Description of services: The Society is an independent trade union, representing writers' interests in all aspects of the writing profession, including publishing, broadcasting, television and films, theatre and translation and has now 300 members in Scotland. It has specialist groups for broadcasters, literary translators, educational, medical and children's writers and illustrators and technical writers.

SOCIETY OF FREELANCE EDITORS AND PROOFREADERS (SFEP)

Mermaid House, 1 Mermaid Court, London SE1 1HR
Contact: Sue King (Administrative Officer)
Objectives: To promote high editorial standards and achieve recognition of the professional status of its members.
Description of services: The SFEP provides its members with a regular newsletter, an annual national conference, local meetings and a programme of reasonably priced workshops/training sessions. An annual directory of members' services is available to publishers. The Society supports moves towards recognized standards of training and accreditation for editors and proofreaders, and is currently phasing in its own system of accreditation. The SFEP has close links with Book House Training Centre and the Society of Indexers, is represented on the BSI Technical Committee dealing with copy preparation and proof correction (BS 5261), and works to foster good relations with all relevant bodies and organizations in the UK and worldwide.

SOCIETY OF INDEXERS (SCOTTISH GROUP)

Bentfield, 3 Marine Terrace, Gullane, East Lothian EH31 2AY
Tel: 01620 842247
Contact: Anne McCarthy
Objectives: The Scottish Group represents the Society locally. It aims to promote indexing amongst Scottish publishers and authors and to provide a forum for indexers.
Description of services: Contact point for everyone interested in the indexing of books, periodicals and other materials. Meetings and training sessions for members. *Indexers Available in Scotland* is published and circulated regularly; it lists indexers and their specialised subjects.

STANDARD BOOK NUMBERING AGENCY LTD

12 Dyott Street, London WC1A 1DF
Tel: 0171 420 6000
Fax: 0171 836 4342
Contact: Lars Andreasen (Manager)
Objectives: The Standard Book Numbering Agency Ltd is the national ISBN agency for the UK and the Republic of Ireland.
Description of services: The Agency issues new publishers joining the scheme with a publisher identifier. Where appropriate the Agency also creates, records and verifies individual ISBNs.

WOMEN IN PUBLISHING SCOTLAND

c/o Larousse plc, 7 Hopetoun Crescent, Edinburgh EH7 4AY
Tel: 0131 556 5929
Fax: 0131 556 5313
Contact: Ilona Bellos-Morison
Objectives: A forum for all women interested or involved in the book industry to provide support (training, advice) and discuss relevant issues. Non-members are welcome.
Description of services: Monthly meetings with a guest speaker, first Thursday of each month (except August) held at Lister Housing, 36 Lauriston Place at 7.30pm. A newsletter is also issued monthly, reporting meetings, news items and future events (literary lunches, Christmas party).

ORGANISATIONS

Other useful contacts:
Booksellers Association of Great Britain and Ireland, *Minster House, 272 Vauxhall Bridge Road, London, SW1V 1BA. Tel: 0171 834 5477. Fax: 0171 834 8812.*

Libray Association, *7 Ridgmount Street, London, WC1E 7AE. Tel: 0171 636 5375. Fax: 0171 436 7218.*

Public Lending Right, *Bayheath House, Prince Regent Street, Stockton-on-Tees, Cleveland TS18 1DF. Tel: 01642 604699. Fax: 01642 615641.*

The Publishers Association, *19 Bedford Square, London WC1B 3HJ. Tel: 0171 580 6321. Fax: 0171 636 5375.*

School Libary Association in Scotland, *Cathryn Buckham, Peebles High School, Springwood Road, Peebles EH45 9HB. Tel: 01721 720291*

SERVICES

GENERAL

DAVID ALBURY

PO Box 151, Edinburgh EH1 3NN
Tel: 0131 556 4595
Fax: 0131 557 0504 (bureau)
Mobile tel: 0831 263 197
Qualifications and experience: Co-writer of *The Scottish Hotel Guide 1990*; regular crossword compiler; organiser and presenter of pub quizzes; compiler of *The Quizmaster Scottish Quiz Book*, published by Polygon
Equipment: Amstrad PCW 8256, Olivetti/Mentor PC (IBM compatible)
Services offered: Compiling crosswords (general and thematic), setting quizzes, research

DAVID FLETCHER ASSOCIATES

58 John Street, Penicuik, Midlothian EH26 8NE
Tel: 01968 673409
Fax: 01968 675723
Qualifications and experience: David Fletcher has been involved in academic, general and professional publishing, books and journals, for over 30 years.
Equipment: Macintosh Performa 6200; WordPerfect; Personal LaserWriter 300
Description of services: The firm offers two unique, high-quality services: 1. Advice on all publishing matters, from product origination, to policy, production, promotion and marketing. 2. The preparation and production of books and journals mainly for academic, learned and professional bodies lacking publishing facilities of their own
Services offered: Advice on all publishing matters; the preparation and production of books and journals

LINDA SPENCE

7 Fishwick Cottages, Nr Paxton, Berwick-Upon-Tweed TD15 1XQ
Tel: 01289 386722
Qualifications and experience: 20 years secretarial. RSA I, II and III typing – shorthand 120 wpm. Book and theses experience.
Equipment: Home-based computer – Amstrad – using Windows and Pressworks II
Description of services: Any kind of typing undertaken, with a professional finish. Work welcomed by post. No work too small or too large.
Services offered: A fast and efficient service with accuracy as the key. Very competitive rates charged. Several authors have had work satisfactorily produced.

EDITORIAL

ROSEMARY ADDISON

4 Duncan Street, Edinburgh EH9 1SZ
Tel: 0131 668 2098
Fax: 0131 667 4173
Qualifications and experience: Freelance since 1985, Diploma in Printing and Publishing, BA
Equipment: Apple Macintosh Performa 630, fax, answerphone
Description of services: Copy-editing, proofreading, project management, typographical design, editorial reading and advice
Services offered: Annual report checking, manuscript reading and preparation. Production and editorial services

KATE BLACKADDER

39 Warrender Park Terrace, Edinburgh EH9 1EB
Tel/fax: 0131 228 4237
Qualifications and experience: 21 years' publishing experience in-house and freelance in London and Edinburgh
Description of services: Manuscript assessment; creative copy-editing; proofreading on general, non-fiction, fiction and children's titles. Book reviews.
Services offered/previous clients: Clients include Scottish Arts Council, Scottish Equitable, Scottish Children's Press, Canongate Books. Private creative copy-editing commissions also undertaken.

ALISON BOWERS

49 Mayfield Road, Edinburgh EH9 2NQ
Tel: 0131 667 8317
Qualifications and experience: Hons English degree. Five years' experience on Pergamon/Elsevier linguistics encyclopedia: commissioning, author–editor liaison, editing, writing, translation (French). Medical textbook project-editing from original manuscript via all stages to collation.
Equipment: Portable Compaq computer, Word software
Description of services: Project editing: author liaison, copy-editing all stages. Proofreading English, French, Spanish. Subject areas: all literary/humanities, linguistics, medicine.

MARGARET CHRISTIE

18 Tay Street, Edinburgh EH11 1EB
Tel: 0131 228 3990
Qualifications and experience: BA in Music; Registered Indexer. Over fifteen years' experience as publishing freelance.
Description of services: Copy-editing and proofreading (including sheet music); language editing; indexing. Arts and social subjects covered.

DEBBIE DOUGRAY

118 McDonald Road, Edinburgh EH7 4NQ
Tel/fax: 0131 556 4876
Qualifications and experience: BA, Diploma in Book and
Periodical Publishing, TEFL (Distinction) Certificate. Over 13 years'
experience working as a copy-editor and proofreader in a full-time
capacity, and extensive freelance experience.
Equipment: IBM PC compatible using Windows 95. Lotus
Smartsuite 96: Wordpro (previously AMIPRO), Lotus 123 and Lotus
Approach. Microsoft Office: Word for Windows (ver. 7), Excel (ver.
7), Powerpoint. GPS Suite: Pressworks Desktop Publishing (ver. 2),
Designworks (ver. 3). Fax/modem 28800 bps. Laser printer,
photocopier.
Services offered: Proofreading and copy-editing for the following:
books (educational, children's, fiction, non-fiction); catalogues;
diaries; pamphlets; periodicals; brochures; calendars, recipe books,
advertising literature. Corporate: financial, marketing, in-house
magazines, newsletters, training, investment, legal, technical, life
assurance-related literature.

BILL HOUSTON

45 Bridge Street, Musselburgh, Midlothian EH21 6AA
Tel: 0131 665 7825
Qualifications and experience: BSc (Hons), DipLib, MPhil,
Chartered Biologist, 20 years' experience
Description of services: Comprehensive editorial service, from
manuscript preparation through to final proofs, including collation.
All-year-round service. Specialist in medical and scientific texts.
Originally sub-editor with Elsevier in Amsterdam; 20 years'
experience as a full-time freelance editor.
Services offered/previous clients: Sub-editing, proofreading, re-
writing, abstracting, book reviewing. Numerous clients throughout
the UK.

ALISON J. IRVING

3 Danskin Place, Strathkinness, St Andrews, Fife KY16 9XN
Tel/fax: 01334 850676
Qualifications and experience: B.Ed History, member of Society of
Freelance Editors and Proofreaders. Introduction to Proofreading
course, teacher of English
Equipment: Word processor
Description of services: Proofreading, re-writing, reduction of text,
writing
Services offered/previous clients: Scripture Union, Whittles
Publishing Services – proofreading and text reduction. Particular
interest in history, biography, children's books and Christian books.

DEREK MANSON-SMITH

Information Research Consultancy, 4 Cleveden Drive, Glasgow G12 0SE

Tel/fax: 0141 334 2724

Qualifications and experience: PhD (London); research consultancy, writing and technical editing in economic development, consumer, local and central government, legal, reference and public-sector issues.

Equipment: 486 PC with WordPerfect 5.2 for Windows and HP laser printer

Description of services: Research, writing and technical editing

Services offered/previous clients: Author of publications including *Moving House in Scotland, The Legal System in Scotland* (HMSO/ Scottish Consumer Council). Have previously worked with the Scottish Consumer Council, European Communications Policy Research Group, Peter Gibson Associates, HMSO and The Scottish Community Education Council.

STEPHANIE PICKERING

95 Spottiswoode Street, Edinburgh EH9 1BZ

Tel/fax: 0131 447 9690

Qualifications and experience: BA (Hons) French and European Literature, MA Librarianship. Employed in publishing, libraries, bookselling and have freelance experience in these areas.

Equipment: Apple Macintosh computer and printer; Microsoft Word; fax machine

Services offered: Editing, including on-screen; cataloguing; proofreading; indexing; research; copy writing; re-writing; translation (French/English) and interpreting. Subject areas include: reference and other non-fiction (natural history, history, geography, sociology, architecture); medicine; literary biography and literature; children's.

RONNIE SCOTT

11 Belhaven Terrace, Glasgow G12 0TG

Tel/fax: 0141 334 9577

E-mail: ronniescott@tintin.demon.co.uk

Qualifications and experience: BA English, 18 years in media, National Union of Journalists and British Association of Communicators in Business (BACB) member. BACB Scotland Editor of the Year 1994.

Equipment: Apple Macintosh Centris 650 CD, Apple Macintosh colour scanner and Laserwriter, full Internet connection, QuarkXpress, Word

Description of services: Writing, re-writing, ghost-writing, editing, video script-writing, desktop publishing, newsletter and newspaper editing and design

Services offered: Full editorial and production services

DOROTHY MITCHELL SMITH

5 Saxe Coburg Street, Edinburgh EH3 5BN
Tel/fax: 0131 556 2928 (answer machine)
and 44 Brentham Way, Ealing, London W5 1BE
Tel: 0181 997 4580 (answer machine)
Fax: 0181 840 3566 (bureau)
Qualifications and experience: In-house and freelance since 1970;
Dip Cert Ed; National Vocational Qualification (NVQ) Assessor
Equipment: IBM compatible PC with WordPerfect 5.1 and Word for
Windows 6.0
Description of services: Total editorial package including editing on
screen. Subject areas include art, architecture, archaeology,
education (primary/middle school), travel, leisure and academic
(principally arts, but some science). Book House Training Centre
and Society of Freelance Editors and Proofreaders tutor in copy-
editing skills.
Services offered: Project management, copy-editing, picture
research, proofreading, training, NVQ assessment

ADRIAN T. SUMNER

35 West Street, Penicuik, Midlothian EH26 9DG
Tel/fax: 01968 672265
Qualifications and experience: MA, DPhil, regular copy-editing
since going freelance in 1995; occasional indexing over more than
25 years.
Equipment: IBM-compatible PC, with MS-DOS 6.22, Word for
Windows 6, Excel 5.0, Macrex 6 (indexing program)
Services offered: Copy-editing, indexing, abstracting, re-writing.
Specialising in biomedicine (especially genetics and cell biology).

LITERARY AGENT

DUNCAN McARA

28 Beresford Gardens, Edinburgh EH5 3ES
Tel/fax: 0131 552 1558
Qualifications and experience: Diploma in Publishing; General
Commissioning Editor, John Murray (1976–88); Assistant Editor,
Faber & Faber (1972–76)
Description of services: Editing, re-writing, copy-editing, proof
correction for wide range of UK publishers. Literary agent for thrillers
and literary fiction; non-fiction: art, architecture, archaeology,
biography, film, military, travel (home 10%, overseas by arrangement).
Preliminary letter with SAE essential. No reading fee.
Services offered: Editorial consultant on all aspects of trade
publishing; literary agent

WRITING

RENNIE McOWAN
7 Williamfield Avenue, Stirling FK7 9AH
Tel: 01786 461316
Qualifications and experience: Writer, broadcaster, lecturer, tutor.
Degrees from Open University, F.S.A. Scot.
Description of services: Freelance writing, articles, scripts, books.
Public relations advice and strategy. Research. Subjects include:
environment, history, religion, tourism, creative writing.

INDEXING

CHARLES S. COVENTRY
27/1 Jamaica Mews, Edinburgh EH3 6HL
Tel: 0131 225 9414
Qualifications and experience: MA, BPhil, MLitt, Dip TEFL.
Experienced in proofreading, indexing both Gaelic and English
Equipment: VTECH 486 DX 2-50 computer AMI-PRO
Description of services: Indexing, books, humanities, newspapers,
proofreading, copy-editing
Services offered/previous clients: SAP index; *Old Town and South
Side News*, index; NBS proofreading (Gaelic); EUP proofreading,
Gaelic; Howard Associates, proofreading guide on English; Korean
law students, proofreading theses.

PETER B. GUNN
Ben-y-Home, Dundas Street, Comrie, Crieff, Perthshire PH6 2LN
Tel/Fax: 01764 670314
Qualifications and experience: BA (Hons) Dip Ed. Member of
Society of Indexers. Over 6 years' experience full-time indexing.
Equipment: Computer indexing program (IBM compatible). Disk
files provided (ASCII).
Description of services: Indexing of books and journals:
archaeology, history, military and aviation, history, education,
maritime topics.
Previous clients: *After the Battle* books and journal, LLP Ltd,
Council for British Archaeology

CHANTAL HAMILL

128 Gowanbank, Livingston, West Lothian EH54 6EW
Tel: 01506 413554
Fax: 0131 225 8329
Qualifications and experience: Maitrise-es-Lettres (Paris-VIII), Dip Lib
Equipment: PC and specialised indexing program. Indexes supplied on disk.
Description of services: Indexing
Services offered: Books and periodicals – extensive experience in law indexing – other specialist subjects include: history – French and French culture.

INDX LTD

No. 3 Coast, Inverasdale, Poolewe, Achnasheen, Ross-shire IV22 1LR
Tel: 01445 781438
and
Heatherknowe, Blairs, Aberdeen AB12 5YA
Tel: 01224 781043
E-mail: 100265.2771@compuserv.com
Qualifications and experience: All indexers working for Indx Ltd are qualified with the Society of Indexers.
Equipment: PC with standard Windows set-up and specialised indexing software
Description of services: Indexes provided for books, journals, technical manuals and web pages

ANNE McCARTHY

Bentfield, 3 Marine Terrace, Gullane, East Lothian EH31 2AY
Tel/fax: 01620 842247
Qualifications and experience: MA, ALA, registered indexer, over 20 years' experience
Equipment: Specialised computer-indexing program. Disks provided (IBM compatible)
Description of services: Indexing
Services offered: Small or large indexes undertaken. Particular interests: medical sciences, Scottish history and culture, local history, sport, travel and guidebooks, biography and reference works.

PUBLICITY

JAN RUTHERFORD

5 West Stanhope Place, Roseburn, Edinburgh EH12 5HQ
Tel/fax: 0131 337 9724

Qualifications and experience: Diploma in Book and Periodical Publishing (1984); twelve years of experience in the promotion, publicity and sales departments of publishing houses in Scotland and London; lecturing experience at Napier University, Edinburgh – three years part-time lecturing in book marketing.

Equipment: Apple Macintosh desktop publishing system, laser printing and scanning facilities

Services offered: Promotional campaigns (media interviews, press coverage, direct mail and advertising) tailored to an individual author or to a publisher's list. Publicity jacket mailings and preparation of review lists. Sponsorship investigation. Catalogues, advance information sheets and press releases written and designed; promotional print-buying and design/illustration commissioning services offered. Also newsletters and in-house magazines written, edited and designed.

Previous clients: The Amaising Publishing House, Birlinn, Book Trust Scotland (The McVitie's Prize), Canongate Books, Chambers (Larousse plc), David & Charles, Jiig-Cal Careers Resource Centre, Napier University, Neil Wilson Publishing Ltd, Phipps PR (The Famous Grouse Finest Scotch Whisky) and Pookie Prouctions

DESIGN AND ILLUSTRATION

MARK BLACKADDER

39 Warrender Park Terrace, Edinburgh EH9 1EB
Tel/fax: 0131 228 4237
Qualifications and experience: Diploma in Art and Design.
Eighteen years graphic design experience, of which the last six and a
half as freelance.
Equipment: Apple Macintosh using QuarkXpress, Photoshop.
Scanner and optical disk drive.
Description of services: The internal and external design of books and
promotional material. From initial roughs through to final disk artwork.
Previous clients: The Amaising Publishing House, ASLS, Birlinn,
Book Trust Scotland, Canongate Books, T&T Clark, Edinburgh
University Press, W. Green, Health Education Board for Scotland,
Mercat Press, National Library of Scotland, National Museums of
Scotland, Neil Wilson Publishing Ltd, Saint Andrew Press, Scottish
Arts Council, Scottish Cultural Press and Tuckwell Press.

DOUGLAS DOUGAN

DD Design, 3 Lower Joppa, Portobello, Edinburgh EH15 2ER
Tel/fax: 0131 669 0046
E-mail: 101337.1247@compuserve.com
Qualifications and experience: Ten years' experience both in-house
and freelance
Equipment: Fully computerised design using Word, PageMaker and
Photoshop. 1200dpi flatbed colour scanner. 1000dpi black and white
and colour output.
Description of services: Comprehensive design package for books,
catalogues, magazines, journals and other printed material.
Services offered/previous clients: Award-winning services: quality
at a sensible price. Everything from initial brief to design and
finished artwork. Clients include: Historic Scotland, BT, Edinburgh
Chamber, plus a range of corporate and commercial publishers.

SHONA GRANT

565 Shields Road, Pollockshields, Glasgow, Strathclyde G41 2RW
Tel: 0141 423 4853
Qualifications and experience: 10 years working as a freelance in
both London and Scotland
Description of services: Book illustration for most subjects. Colour
(gouache, watercolour, pen and wash) and black and white (ink, line,
scraperboard).
Services offered/previous clients: General, children's and medical
illustrations. Clients include Heinemann, Michael Joseph, Cassell,
Butterworths, Souvenir Press, Christopher Helm, Blackies, Elm Tree
Books, Simon & Schuster, Walker Books, Macmillan.

RIVER DESIGN CONSULTANCY, THE

4–6 Coltbridge Avenue, Murrayfield, Edinburgh EH12 6AH
Tel: 0131 467 7702
Fax: 0131 337 5999
Qualifications and experience: Fully accredited and qualified designers with extensive experience in the design for print/ publishing industries
Equipment: Two PowerMacs 7100, 230MB optical drive, flatbed colour scanner and colour printer. Software includes QuarkXpress, Adobe Photoshop, Illustrator, Dimensions and Super Paint
Description of services: Assignments range from book jacket design and illustration to corporate identities, brochures and other sales literature.
Services offered/previous clients: A complete design service is provided from high quality colour visuals to finished artwork on disk. Reprographics and print management services also offered as required. Client list includes Blackwell Publishers, Churchill Livingstone, Edinburgh University Press, Geddes & Grosset, Neil Wilson Publishing Ltd, Penguin Books, Polygon, W. Green.

SHAUN McLAREN

Flat 1, 8 Kelvin Drive, Glasgow G20 8QG
Tel/fax: 0141 945 2826
Qualifications and experience: BA (Hons) Graphic Design (1987). Freelance illustrator since October 1994.
Equipment: Variety of mediums for producing artwork plus Apple Macintosh computer for occasional design work.
Description of services: Full colour and black and white illustrations for books, magazines, advertisements. Several different styles. Arrange appointment to view portfolio.
Previous clients: BBC Scotland, *Scotland on Sunday*, Neil Wilson Publishing Ltd, *The List*, *The Big Issue Scotland*, British Telecom, British Aerospace, Edinburgh District Council.

ANN ROSS PATERSON

9 Craiglea Place, Edinburgh EH10 5QA
Tel/fax: 0131 447 3183
Qualifications and experience: DA (Edin); in publishing since 1972, in-house and freelance
Equipment: PowerMac, Nikon scanner, A3 colour printer. Software includes QuarkXpress, Freehand and Photoshop
Description of services: Graphic design, illustration, illustrated maps for publications or packaging
Services offered: All design from consultancy to finished artwork. Clients include Edinburgh Book Festival, Book Trust Scotland, Floris Books, Faber and Faber

JANET WATSON

Unit 4, Wellpark Enterprise Centre, 110 Sydney Street, Glasgow
G31 1JF
Tel: 0141 550 4994
Fax: 0141 550 4443
Qualifications and experience: City and Guilds in Design for
Publishing, City and Guilds in Desktop Publishing, over 15 years'
experience working in Scotland and London
Equipment: PowerMac running QuarkXpress, Illustrator,
Photoshop. Syquest optical drive, colour scanner and colour printer
Description of services: A complete service from concept to
finished artwork, including commissioning and print liaison
Services offered/previous clients: Cover design, page layout,
catalogues and promotional material. Clients include Birlinn, EUP,
Hodder & Stoughton, Lindsay Publications, NMS, NWP, Whittles
Publishing.

STEVE WHELAN

Graphics & Co, Raemartin Cottage, Main Street, West Linton,
Peeblesshire EH46 7EA
Tel: 01968 660197
Fax: 01968 660942
Qualifications and experience: LSIA, Scottish Borders Enterprise
SFDP Registered Design Consultant. 18 years design experience on
brochures, newsletters, corporate identity, stationery, advertisements,
packaging and exhibition stands.
Equipment: PowerMac 7500, AGFA scanner, SyQuest 200MB
drive. Software: QuarkXpress, Freehand, Photoshop, Painter,
Deltagraph, Barcoda.
Description of services: Full service from initial brief to design,
artwork and print liaison, where required
Previous clients: Blackwell Scientific Publications, Frame of Mind
Publishing, Scottish Publishers Association, The University of
Edinburgh

CARTOGRAPHY

DAVID LANGWORTH

Allan Lodge, Pavilion, Melrose TD6 9BN
Tel: 01896 822823
Qualifications and experience: Diploma in Cartography;
Cartographic Editor (in-house) with map publishers; freelance
cartography for nine years.
Equipment: Apple Macintosh PowerMac 7200/90; Image Scanner
and colour ink-jet printer. Freehand, Photoshop and word processing/
DTP software.
Description of services: Traditional and computer generated
cartographic artwork; editorial work for publishers including copy-
editing.
Services offered/previous clients: Maps designed and drawn, large
or small scale for travel guides/books; tourist/local authority maps;
Scotland – historical and leisure publishing (walking, cycling, riding
route guides); page layout and compilation for educational and
reference atlases; landscape perspective maps.

JAMES RENNY

Braeriach, Drum, by Kinross KY13 7UL
Tel: 01577 840494
Qualifications and experience: Over 20 years' experience in
diagrammatic cartography. Work has appeared in over 40 separate
publications covering several publishers. An associate of the Royal
Photographic Society (ARPS) with over 30 years' experience in
photography resulting in work being published regularly. Fully
trained and experienced lecturer.
Equipment: General graphic equipment; Nikon cameras with a
range of lenses
Description of services: Diagrammatic cartography in colour and
black and white; map consultancy sketching and general graphic
work. Photographs offered from an extensive library of Scottish
landscape. Mountain landscape a speciality. Illustrated lectures on a
variety of topics.
Services offered: Cartography, photography, lecturing and slide
presentation

PHOTOGRAPHY & PHOTO LIBRARIES

WALTER BELL
Bell Photography, 78 Thirlestane Road, Edinburgh EH9 1AR
Tel: 0131 447 9827
Qualifications and experience: BSc LRPS, several years carrying
out photographic work for established publishers and graphic artists
Equipment: 35mm, 6x6 and 6x7cm medium formats, 5x4 large format
Description of services: High quality photography in-house and
location. Colour and monochrome in all formats.
Previous clients: Saint Andrew Press, Mercat Press, Canongate
Books, Health Education Board, Knox Press, Scottish Arts Council,
Scottish Academic Press, Scottish Cultural Press

IMAGE BANK
14 Alva Street, Edinburgh EH2 4QG
Tel: 0131 225 1770
Fax: 0131 225 1660
Description of services: Photo library
Services offered: Provider of still photography, illustrations, film
footage, to advertising, publishing arena

SUE OSMOND PHOTOGRAPHY
1/9 Forrest Hill, Edinburgh EH1 2QL
Tel: 0131 225 1009
Mobile tel: 0976 401057
Qualifications and experience: BA (Hons) in Photography, Film
and Television. Experienced freelance photographer, portfolio
available on request.
Equipment: All formats in studio and on location
Description of services: Documentary, editorial, advertising,
portraiture and film stills
Previous clients: *Scotland on Sunday*, *The Scotsman*, Shelter Scotland,
Classical Music Magazine, Edinburgh University, Macbeth plc

DAVID WILLIAMS PICTURE LIBRARY
50 Burlington Avenue, Glasgow G12 0LH
Tel: 0141 339 7823
Fax: 0141 337 3031
Qualifications and experience: Eleven years' experience of writing
travel books. Eight years' experience of running a picture library.
Member of the British Association of Picture Libraries and Agencies.
Description of services: Supply of medium format and 35mm
colour transparencies of Scotland and Iceland. Subjects include
towns, villages, landscapes, historical buildings. Commissions
undertaken. Catalogue available. Travel books and articles written.
Services offered: Supply of colour transparencies for reproduction

DAVID GREGOR

Derek Walker Partnership, 40 Porterfield, Comrie, Dunfermline, Fife
KY12 9HJ
Tel/fax: 01383 850778
Qualifications and experience: Considerable experience
representing general, academic and specialist publishers calling on
bookshops, wholesalers, library suppliers and specialist outlets.
Description of services: Publishers' agent in Scotland in association
with Derek Walker whose area is Northern England
Services offered: Sales representation, marketing and limited
distribution

BRIAN PUGH

Flat 11, 50 Craighouse Gardens, Edinburgh EH10 5TZ
Tel/fax: 0131 452 8431
Qualifications and experience: Eighteen years experience in the
book trade: 9 years as a buyer, 9 years as a publishers' representative
Description of services: Representation to the book trade in
Scotland, North-East England and Ireland

SEOL LTD

14 High Street, Edinburgh EH1 1TE
Tel/fax: 0131 558 1500
Qualifications and experience: Company comprises: Hugh
Andrew, Carol Crawford and John Lennie
Services offered: Representation to the trade in Scotland. The only
sales force to cover Scotland from Shetland to Stranraer with three
of the most experienced reps in the Scottish trade. Most extensive
customer base of any sales force outside wholesale.

SERVICES

BOOKSPEED

62 Hamilton Place, Edinburgh EH3 5AZ
Tel: 0131 225 4950
Fax: 0131 220 6515
Company established: 1986
Contacts: Annie Rhodes and Kingsley Dawson (Joint Managing Directors)
Services offered: Wholesaling of books to retail book trade, gift shops, visitor centres. Four reps cover Scotland.
Description of services: Over 20,000 titles carried, next day delivery provided, new title subscription service and advice on stock ranges. Help is available on shelving. Attendance at all appropriate trade shows. *See display advert below*.

LIBRARY SUPPLY

T. C. FARRIES AND CO. LTD
Irongray Road, Lochside, Dumfries DG2 0LH
Tel: 01387 720755
Fax: 01387 721105
Company established: 1981
Contacts: Linda Bennett (Sales and Purchasing Director)
Services offered: One of the UK's leading library suppliers of books, audio–visual material and information products.
Description of services: Suppliers of books, audio–visual materials, bibliographic data, pre-publication information, weekly approval collections, multi-copy stocks, mobile and trailer services, library processing and delivery.

PRINT/PRODUCTION

ANTONY ROWE LTD
Bumper's Farm, Chippenham, Wiltshire SN14 6LH
Tel: 01249 659705
Fax: 01249 443103
E-mail: 100616.40@compuserve.com
Company established: 1983
Contact: Ian Hilder (Sales Director)
Services offered: Book, journal and looseleaf; limp and cased; finishing: sewn, unsewn and notched.
Description of services: Short-run and on-demand book, journal and looseleaf manufacture.

THE IPSWICH BOOK COMPANY
The Drift, Nacton Road, Ipswich, Suffolk IP3 9QR
Tel: 01473 711144
Fax: 01473 271412
Company established: 1989
Contacts: Jonathan Boughey (Commercial Director); Julie Walker (Business Development Manager)
Services offered: *See display advertisement overleaf*

REDWOOD BOOKS
23 Bedford Square, London WC1B 3HH
Tel: 0171 580 9328
Fax: 0171 580 9337
Contacts: John Morris; Keith Kirkland
Services offered: See display advertisement overleaf

THE CROMWELL PRESS
Broughton Gifford, Melksham, Wiltshire SN12 8PH
Tel: 01225 782585
Fax: 01225 782659
Contact: John Turner
Services offered: *See display advertisement overleaf*

REDWOOD
BOOKS

Redwood Books has been manufacturing books for
twenty-nine years and prides itself on the high level
of quality and customer service.

———————•———————

We produce books in a variety of syles and formats for over
350 publishers each year and have a continuing programme
of investment to ensure we provide the fast turnaround
and economic production our customers require.

———————•———————

For a brochure and further information please contact
our London sales office.

Manufacturing Site

Kennet Way
Trowbridge
Wiltshire BA14 8RN

Tel: 01225 769979
Fax: 01225 769050

London Sales Office

22 Bloomsbury Square
London
WC1A 2NS

Tel: 0171 580 9328
Fax: 0171 580 9337

WRITING
Getting published

The typescript

In previous years, it has been acceptable for would-be authors to present their work to a publisher in the form of a manuscript. With the increase in the use of computers and word-processors, however, publishers are very reluctant to read through long-hand, unsolicited works, so anything presented to a publisher should be in a typed form. Typescripts should be easy to handle and read and complete in all details. The typescript, therefore, should fulfil the following requirements:

- It should be typed on one side of the paper, double-spaced throughout with generous margins.
- The pages should be numbered throughout. Late additions should be typed on separate sheets and slotted into the typescript, these too should be numbered e.g.10a. You should indicate on page 10 that page 10a follows.
- A4 sized paper should be used.
- Illustrations and/or diagrams should be separate from the typescript and each one numbered for identification, with captions and corresponding numbers typed together on a separate sheet.

The above points are only general guidelines and each publishing house will have its own house style giving detailed instructions on presentation and editorial style. The house style of any publisher should be followed *exactly*.

Sending the typescript to a publisher

If the typescript is unsolicited, it is important, once the typescript is complete, that it is sent to appropriate publishers. Much time and money can be wasted in not carrying out sufficient research into specific publishers' lists. It is unlikely that a publisher would alter their publishing practice on the strength of an unsolicited typescript. *The Writers' and Artists' Yearbook* lists publishers and their addresses together with a brief description of the types of book each company publishes, as does the first section of this directory. These are intended to be very rough guides so it is often good to browse in a bookshop or library to find publishers of the type of book you have written.

When you have a list of suitable publishers, write to them asking whether you may submit your work. Do not send your typescript direct to the publishers as it will automatically be added to the 'slush' pile and may not be read for many weeks. Tell the publisher *briefly* what your work is about, what market it is aimed at, its unique selling points (very important in today's saturated market) and perhaps send a small sample section. Also tell the publisher about any relevant qualifications and experience which you have. Be brief and be business-like. Send a stamped-addressed-envelope with your initial enquiry – make it as easy as possible for the publisher to reply to you. If the publisher is willing to consider your typescript, send them a *copy* (keep hold of the original) together with postage for its return. It may take some time for the publisher to get around to reading your typescript so try to be patient!

Further information on writing and presentation of work to publishers can be found in the 'Writing' section of the bibliography on p. 118.

See also: *Author–Publisher Network p. 67*
         Scottish Arts Council p. 55
         The Society of Authors in Scotland p. 71

Other useful addresses:
Arvon at Moniak Mhor, *Teavarron, Kiltarlity, Beauly, Invernssh-shire IV4 7HT. Tel: 01463 741675*

Scottish Society of Playrights, *c/o Netherbow Arts Centre, 43 High Street, Edinburgh EH1 1SR. Tel: 0131 556 8093*

Writers Guild, *Alison Thirkell, 30 Mortonhall Park Avenue, Edinburgh EH17 8BP*

Prizes and Awards

AGNES MURE MACKENZIE AWARD, THE

The Saltire Society, 9 Fountain Close, 22 High Street, Edinburgh
EH1 1TF
Tel: 0131 556 1836
Fax: 0131 557 1675
Final entry date: 31st January 1997
Presentation date: March 1997
Value: Amount varies
Frequency: Biennially, by nomination from publishers and from
professors of Scottish history
Description: For a published work of Scottish historical research
(including intellectual history and the history of science)

DUNDEE BOOK PRIZE, THE

Press Office, University of Dundee, Dundee DD1 4HN
Tel: 01382 344021   **Fax**: 01382 345515
and
Beattie Media, Prospect House, Technology Park, Dundee
Tel: 01382 598408   **Fax**: 01382 598442
Final entry date: 31st May 1998
Presentation date: August/September 1998
Prize value: £5,000 and probable publication
Frequency: One prize initially but if successful it is hoped to present
the prize every two years
Description of award: The Dundee Book Prize is a new prize for an
unpublished novel set in Dundee past or present. Entry is free and
open to all via the official entry form. Launched by the University of
Dundee in association with the Dundee Partnership as part of the
City of Discovery Campaign. The prize has the support of the
publisher, Polygon, who are committed to publishing the winning
novel – assuming it is of publishable standard.

FIDLER AWARD, THE

c/o Book Trust Scotland, Scottish Book Centre, 137 Dundee Street,
Edinburgh EH11 1BG
Tel: 0131 229 3663
Fax: 0131 228 4293
Final entry date: 31st October
Presentation date: October the following year
Value: £1,000 and guaranteed publication
Frequency: Annual competitive
Description: For a novel of 20,000–25,000 words for children aged
8–12 years. Authors should not previously have had a novel
published for this age group. The award is sponsored by Hodder
Children's Books and administered by Book Trust Scotland. The
winning entry will be published by Hodder Children's Books.

WRITING

95

JAMES TAIT BLACK MEMORIAL PRIZES

University of Edinburgh, Department of English Literature, David Hume Tower, George Square, Edinburgh EH8 9JX
Tel: 0131 650 3619
Final entry date: 30th September
Presentation date: February
Value: Two prizes of £3,000 each
Frequency: Annual competitive
Description: One prize for fiction and one for biography, or work of that nature, first published in Britain in the previous 12 months. Supplemented by the Scottish Arts Council since 1979.

MACALLAN/*SCOTLAND ON SUNDAY* SHORT STORY COMPETITION, THE

The Administrator, The Macallan/*Scotland on Sunday* Short Story Competition, 20 North Bridge, Edinburgh EH1 1YT
Tel: 0131 243 3344
Fax: 0131 220 2443
Final entry date: 1st April
Presentation date: June
Value: First prize: £6,000 and publication in *Scotland on Sunday*; second prize: £600 and four runners-up receive £100 each
Frequency: Annual competitive
Description: Aimed at finding the best short story writer in Scotland. The maximum length for each short story is 3,000 words and up to three stories may be submitted. Stories must not have been previously submitted to this competition, published, performed or read on the radio. Entries are accepted from anyone born in Scotland, persons resident in Scotland and Scots living abroad.

MCVITIE'S PRIZE FOR THE SCOTTISH WRITER OF THE YEAR, THE

c/o Book Trust Scotland, Scottish Book Centre, 137 Dundee Street, Edinburgh EH11 1BG
Tel: 0131 229 3663   **Fax**: 0131 228 4293
Final entry date: 31st July
Presentation date: November
Value: Scottish Writer of the Year: £10,000. Four other shortlisted writers: £1,000.
Frequency: Annual by nomination
Description: For the best substantial work of an imaginative nature first published, performed, filmed or transmitted between 1st August and 31st July. Novels, collections of short stories, volumes of poetry, biography, autobiography, children's fiction, non-fiction, journalism and theatre, cinema, radio and television scripts are all eligible. Writers must be born in Scotland, or have Scottish parents, or have been resident in Scotland for a considerable period, or take Scotland as their inspiration. Submissions accepted in Scots, English and Gaelic.

C. B. OLDMAN PRIZE, THE

Mr R. Turbet, Aberdeen University Library, Queen Mother Library, Meston Walk, Aberdeen AB24 3UE
Tel: 01224 272592
Presentation date: Easter
Value: £150
Frequency: Annual competitive
Description: Awarded by UK branch of the International Association of Music Libraries for the year's best book of music bibliography, librarianship or reference by an author domiciled in UK.

SALTIRE SOCIETY SCOTTISH LITERARY AWARDS, THE

The Saltire Society, 9 Fountain Close, 22 High Street, Edinburgh EH1 1TF
Tel: 0131 556 1836
Fax: 0131 557 1675
Final entry date: End of August
Presentation date: 30th November
Value: Scottish Book of the Year: £5,000. Scottish First Book of the Year by a New Author: £1,500.
Frequency: Annual by nomination
Description: For a book on or about Scotland, or for a book with Scottish connections, not necessarily written by a Scot. The Scottish Book of the Year is sponsored by *The Scotsman* and the Scottish First Book of the Year is sponsored by the Scottish Post Office Board. Nominations made by literary editors.

SCOTTISH ARTS COUNCIL BOOK AWARDS, THE

Shonagh Irvine, Literature Department, Scottish Arts Council, 12 Manor Place, Edinburgh EH3 7DD
Tel: 0131 226 6051
Fax: 0131 225 9833
Value: £1,000
Frequency: Biannual (spring and autumn)
Description: Five awards are given biannually to new and established authors of published books in recognition of high standards of writing. Authors should be Scottish, resident in Scotland or have published books of Scottish interest. Entries from publishers only.

SCOTTISH BOOK MARKETING GROUP CONTRIBUTION AWARD – TRADE

Scottish Book Marketing Group, Scottish Book Centre, 137 Dundee Street, Edinburgh EH11 1BG
Tel: 0131 228 6866
Fax: 0131 228 3220
Final entry date: June, nominations; September, shortleet
Presentation date: October, at Scottish Book Fortnight launch party
Frequency: Annual by nomination
Award recipient 1996: James Thin Ltd, South Bridge, Edinburgh.
Description: Introduced by the Scottish Book Marketing Group (SBMG) in 1994 in recognition of the continuing development and innovation of the Scottish book trade. This award aims to acknowledge the outstanding contribution made by a nominated group, body or individual, currently working within any area of the Scottish book trade, to the industry. Nominations, the shortleet and the final award recipient are voted for and determined by members of the trade only (including SBMG booksellers, Scottish Publishers Association member publishers and Scottish librarians). Sponsored by BPC Books and Information. *See also p. 44.*

SCOTTISH INTERNATIONAL OPEN POETRY COMPETITION

c/o The Secretary, 42 Tollerton Drive, Irvine, Ayrshire KA12 0QE
Tel: 01294 276381
Final entry date: 31st December
Presentation date: March
Value: £100 and MacDiarmid Trophy (UK section); International Trophy (International section); The Clement Wilson Trophy (Scots section). Diplomas are awarded to runners-up.
Frequency: Annual competitive
Description: The competition was inaugurated in 1972 and is the longest running of its kind in the UK. Entry is free and submissions, limited to two per person, are acceptable from
1st September to 31st December each year. An SAE/International Reply Coupon must accompany entries.

SLOAN PRIZE, UNIVERSITY OF ST ANDREWS

Clerk of the Senate, The University of St Andrews, Fife KY16 9AJ
Tel: 01334 476161
The Sloan Prize is still under review. It is hoped that it will be awarded again in the near future.
The Sloan Prize is awarded for new writing in Scots.

TESS/SALTIRE SOCIETY PRIZE FOR EDUCATIONAL PUBLICATION

The Saltire Society, 9 Fountain Close, 22 High Street, Edinburgh
EH1 1TF
Tel: 0131 556 1836
Fax: 0131 557 1675
Final entry date: End of October
Presentation date: Mid December
Value: £500
Frequency: Annual by nomination
Description: For an example of a published non-fiction work which enhances the teaching and learning of an aspect of the curriculum in Scottish schools. Publications for pre-school age are also being considered.

SCOTTISH CENTRE, INTERNATIONAL PEN

The Honorary Secretary, 33 Drumsheugh
Gardens, Edinburgh EH3 7RN
Tel: 0131 225 1038
Date established: Internationally 1921; Scottish Centre 1927
Contact: Laura Fiorentini, Honorary Secretary

PEN is a writers' association with centres worldwide. It is open to anyone professionally engaged in writing who also subscribes to its aims. The International PEN Charter calls for better understanding and respect between nations through the friendly cooperation of writers, in the interests of freedom of expression throughout the world. PEN is recognised by UNESCO as the voice of the international community of writers. There are more than 120 centres throughout the world. It is one of the very few international organisations, so far, in which Scotland is a full member in its own right.

The Scottish Centre of PEN was established in 1927 on the initiative of Hugh MacDiarmid. Over the years it has included in its membership most of the best-known Scottish writers from Neil Gunn to Alasdair Gray. There are at present about 200 members.

The Scottish Centre holds meetings in Edinburgh and Glasgow during the winter and a summer meeting takes place elsewhere in Scotland. The annual programme includes literary evenings and readings, informal parties for members and guests, invited speakers with expertise of interest to writers, and at least one reception in honour of a visiting writer. In recent years Heinrich Böll, Chinua Achebe, Nadine Gordimer, Brian Moore, Mario Vargas Llosa and Muriel Spark have been guests.

International activities include assistance to writers who have been persecuted or imprisoned for exercising their freedom of expression. On the initiative of the Scottish and Catalan Centres, PEN is now also concerned with linguistic and cultural diversity. This has led to the Universal Declaration of Linguistic Rights approved by a world conference in Barcelona in June 1995 which is likely to enhance the status and support of such languages as Gaelic and Scots.

The international meetings, held each year in a different country, provide an opportunity for writers to exchange views and become friends. International conferences have been held in Scotland on three occasions, most recently in 1970. A full-scale International

PEN Congress will be held in Edinburgh and Glasgow from 5th to 11th August 1997. Approximately 400 participants from about 100 countries are expected. There will be a full programme of discussions, exhibitions and social events. Public literary sessions will be held jointly with the Edinburgh Book Festival. A full-scale PEN Congress of this kind can come to Scotland only about once in a century. It is therefore a unique opportunity to cement international relationships and make Scotland and Scottish writing better known throughout the world.

All published, performed or broadcast writers are welcome to join. The present annual subscription is £20.00 (most of which goes to help finance the international activities of PEN). Application forms can be obtained from the Honorary Secretary at the above address.

WRITING

Literary Journals and Publications

ARTWORK
PO Box 3, Ellon, Aberdeenshire AB41 9EA
Tel: 01651 842429
Fax: 0131 229 6243
E-mail: famedram@artwork.co.uk
Contact: Richard Carr (Editor); Gil Livingston (Advertising)
Title established: 1983
Description of contents: Free arts newspaper for the North of
Scotland

BOOKS IN SCOTLAND
15 Gloucester Place, Edinburgh EH3 6EE
Tel/fax: 0131 225 5646
Contact: Christine Wilson
Publication frequency: Quarterly
Price: £2.25 (subscription for 4 issues £9.95: UK; £10.95: overseas
Description of contents: A comprehensive and stimulating review
of new books by Scottish writers, books about Scotland and books in
general

CENCRASTUS
Unit 1, Abbeymount Techbase, 8 Easter Road, Edinburgh EH8 8EJ
Tel: 0131 661 5687
Contact: Raymond Ross (Editor); Ruth Bradley (Managing Editor)
Title established: 1979
Publication frequency: Quarterly
Price: £2.25
Description of contents: Scottish and international literature, arts
and affairs
Instructions for contributors: Unsolicited material accompanied by
SAE is welcome. Please allow up to eight weeks for a decision to be
made.

CHAPMAN
4 Broughton Place, Edinburgh EH1 3RX
Tel: 0131 557 2207
Fax: 0131 556 9565
Contact: Joy Hendry
Publication frequency: Quarterly
Price: £3.20
Description of contents: Scottish poetry, short stories, articles and
comments on Scottish cultural affairs, reviews. Also international
writing and translations.
Instructions for contributors: Submissions welcome (if
accompanied by SAE). Write for guidelines if in doubt.

THE DARK HORSE

c/o 19 Cunninghamhead Estate, by Kilmarnock, Ayrshire KA3 2PY
Tel: 01294 850348
Contact: Gerry Cambridge (Editor)
Title established: 1995
Publication frequency: Twice yearly, in May/June and October/November
Price: £3.00. Subscription (three issues) £11.00. All cheques payable to 'Dark Horse Writers'
Description of contents: Critical essays and polemic on contemporary poetry; interviews; in-depth reviews; poetry (with an emphasis on work in metre or rhyme; free verse of quality also included).
Instructions for contributors: Essays and reviews usually solicited; writers interested in supplying such material please query first. Poems: four to six poems, with name and address on each page and SAE. Poets should have carefully read the magazine before submitting. Payment: contributors' copy.

EDINBURGH REVIEW

c/o 22 George Square, Edinburgh EH8 9LF
Contact: Robert Alan Jamieson and Gavin Wallace
Title established: 1982
Publication frequency: Twice yearly
Price: £15.75 subscription; £9.50 single copy
Description of contents: Lively, controversial and eclectic, *Edinburgh Review* is the only forum which positively asserts the rich diversity of Scottish arts and culture, while attending to international literary and cultural events.
Instructions for contributors: *Edinburgh Review* is pleased to receive submissions of original fiction, poetry and articles provided they are accompanied by SAE. Please write to the Editors for guidelines regarding submissions.

GAIRFISH

71 Long Lane, Broughty Ferry, Dundee DD5 2AS
Contact: W. N. Herbert or Forbes Browne
Title established: 1989
Publication frequency: Twice yearly
Price: £3.50
Description of contents: Poetry, stories, essays – usually grouped around a theme or themes, for example: Scottish avant-garde, women's issues
Instructions for contributors: Details concerning future issues are announced in each edition's editorial. Due to difficulties in changing production routines, expect some delay in response.

GAIRM

29 Waterloo Street, Glasgow G2 6BZ
Tel/fax: 0141 221 1971
Contact: D. S. Thomson
Title established: 1952
Publication frequency: Quarterly
Price: £1.60/$3.50 (subscription £8.00: UK, £10.00: overseas)
Description of contents: *Gairm* was launched in 1952 and the
summer issue for 1996 was number 175. It is the only all-Gaelic
quarterly in existence, and has subscribers all over the world. *Gairm*
has published over 500 short stories, has done much to lead the
revival of Gaelic poetry in the last 40 years, and deals with all sorts
of contemporary and historical and folklore topics. Special offer of
50-packs of earlier issues are avaiable. Gairm also publish a wide
range of Gaelic books.

LALLANS

c/o The Scots Language Society, A.K. Bell Library, York Place,
Perth PH2 8AP
Tel: 01738 440199
Contact: Neil MacCallum
Publication frequency: Three times a year
Price: £3.00
Description of contents: Articles, stories, critical essays, book
reviews and poems in the Scots language
Instructions for contributors: All contributions must be in the
Scots language, usually in literary Scots although some dialect
material is welcome. Articles should be accompanied by SAE.

LINES REVIEW

Edgefield Road, Loanhead, Midlothian EH20 9SY
Contact: Tessa Ransford
Title established: 1952
Publication frequency: Quarterly
Price: £2.00. Subscription for four issues: £10.00 (UK); £12.00
(overseas)
Description of contents: *Lines Review* has established itself as an
integral part of Scottish literary life, providing a regular opportunity
for the publication of new work and work-in-progress. Although
primarily concerned with the poetry of both new and established
writers, it is also recognised as an important vehicle of contemporary
criticism with a strong international interest, frequently featuring
new writing from abroad.

NEW WRITING SCOTLAND

c/o Dept of Scottish History, 9 University Gardens, University of
Glasgow, Glasgow G12 8QH
Tel: 0141 330 5309
Contact: Catherine McInerney
Title established: 1983
Publication frequency: Annually
Price: £6.95
Description of contents: Contains poetry, prose, drama excerpts and
short stories in Scots, Gaelic, English by new and established writers.
Instructions for contributors: Must be a writer resident in Scotland
or Scots by birth or upbringing. The work must be neither previously
published nor accepted for publication. Submissions should be typed
on one side of the paper only, and should be accompanied by two
SAEs. Deadline for submissions is 31st January of year of publication.

NORTHWORDS

68 Strathkanaird, By Ullapool, Wester Ross IV26 2TW
Tel: 01854 666226
Contact: Tom Bryan (Editor)
Title established: 1991
Publication frequency: 3 times a year
Price: £7.50 per year (3 issues)
Description of contents: Fiction, poetry and reviews in Scots,
Gaelic and English
Instructions for contributors: Poetry submissions are restricted to
five poems; preferred length for stories is 3000 words or less. SAE/
IRC required. Contributors are encouraged to read the magazine
before they submit contributions. Payment is given in copies only.
There is a preference for work from a Highland/Scottish perspective
by writers living in Scotland or exiled. No 'Kailyard' please.

SCOTLANDS

School of English, University of St Andrews, St Andrews KY16 9AL
E-mail: cjmm@edge.st-andrews.ac.uk
Contact: Dr Christopher MacLachlan
Title established: 1994
Publication frequency: Twice yearly
Price: £21.00 subscription; £14.95 single copy
Description of contents: *Scotlands* is an exciting interdisciplinary
journal celebrating the diversity of Scottish culture, reflecting the
views of: historians, literary critics, social scientists, art historians,
musicians and any other profession with something to say about
Scotland past and present.
Instructions for contributors: Scotland, past, present and future.
Articles of up to 6,000 words may be submitted, but authors are
advised to enquire first about the themes planned for future issues.
Please write for guidelines regarding submissions.

WRITING

SCOTTISH BOOK COLLECTOR

c/o 36 Lauriston Place, Edinburgh EH3 9EZ
Tel: 0131 228 4837
Fax: 0131 228 3904
Contact: Jennie Renton (Editor)
Title established: 1987
Publication frequency: Quarterly
Price: £2.50 (annual subscription £11.00: UK)
Description of contents: Articles about collecting books of Scottish interest, from rare, antiquarian items, to contemporary publications; short story with a book collecting theme; author interviews.
Contributors are invited to contact the editor in the first instance.

TOCHER

School of Scottish Studies, 27 George Square, Edinburgh EH8 9LD
Tel: 0131 650 3060
Contact: Fran Beckett (Subscription Secretary)
Title established: 1971
Publication frequency: Biannually
Price: £6.00 (for two issues)
Description of contents: Tales, songs and reminiscences of ordinary and extraordinary people and events throughout the land from Yetholm to St Kilda from the archives of the School of Scottish Studies, opened in 1951. A wide variety of material, in every dialect of Lowland Scots and Scottish Gaelic is included: songs, stories, local legends, music and proverbs, as well as accounts of trades and activities such as fishing, French polishing and weaving.
Translations are provided for all the Galeic and the harder words of Scots and Shetlandic, and staff notation for the traditional songs that are in every issue, and also biographical features and tributes to notable tradition-bearers and collectors. Book and record reviews, and other notes, are included in most issues.

WEST COAST MAGAZINE

Top Floor, 15 Hope Street, Glasgow G2 6AB
Tel/fax: 0141 221 5050
Contact: Joe Murray and Brian Whittingham (Editors)
Title established: 1988
Publication frequency: Three issues per year
Price: £1.98; subscription £10.00 (four issues); £15.00 overseas
subscription or £20.00 if not paid in Sterling; £6.00 unwaged/low
waged (proof required); back issue or single issue £2.50 each
Description of contents:*West Coast Magazine* consists of: short
fiction, poetry, articles, essays and reviews.The magazine's aim is
always to be a platform for mainly new and up and coming, as well
as established, writers.
Instructions for contributors: High quality works from writers who
enjoy a challenge are sought – the quirky and offbeat usually sit well
in the magazine. Pieces should be kept to around 3,500 words –
bigger pieces are published though if the editors are attracted to
them. Sequences of poems, or groups of poems that compliment
each other are welcomed, as are single poems. Any articles of
interest are published, preferably literary interest, but also articles on
football, music, French cinema and public sector housing have
previously been published. Please send SAE with submissions – two
or three short stories and five or six poems (unless, and only, if they
are part of a larger sequence) maximum. Always include cover sheet
with submissions with name, address and title. Name should be
written on each sheet. The magazine always tries to pay a small fee
for work published.

ZED 2 0

Akros Publications, 33 Lady Nairn Avenue, Kirkcaldy, Fife KY1
2AW
Tel: 01592 651 522
Contact: Duncan Glen
Title established: 1991
Publication frequency: Annually
Price: £2.00
Description of contents: An annual magazine with poetry, prose and
articles on literature and the arts.

For details of writing magazines, see p. 110

Writers' Groups

Despite the increasing difficulty which most aspiring writers have in finding a publisher for their work, the number of writers' groups in Scotland is steadily growing. For more information on writers' groups contact your local library or your district council's leisure and recreation department. A fuller list of writers' groups can be found in *High Roads and Low Roads: A Directory for Promoters of Writers' Tours in Scotland* which was published in 1995 by Readiscovery (*for further details, see p. 58*).

Aberdeen Writers' Workshop
Contact: Mr Colin Kilpatrick, 44 Brunswick Place, Aberdeen

Angus Writers' Circle
Contact: Mrs Eileen Ramsay, Bonnyton House, Arbirlot, Arbroath DD11 2PY

Ayr Writers' Club
Contact: Mr A. B. Scott, 7 Seafield Road, Ayr KA7 4AA

Black Isle Writers' Group
Contact: Martin Gostwick, Paye House, Church Street, Cromarty IV11 8XA

Bute Writers' Group
Contact: Arthur Hatfield, 40 East Princes Street, Rothesay, Isle of Bute PA20 9DN

Castlemilk Writers' Workshop
Contact: Ms S. M. Brodie, WEA Rooms, St Margaret Mary's Secondary, Glasgow G45 9NJ

Dumfries Writers' Workshop
Contact: Peter Fortune, 12 Hillview Drive, Dumfries DG1 4DS

Dundee University Writers' Group
Contact: Helen Livingstone, 140 Nethergate, Dundee

Eastwood Writers' Club
Contact: Laura Duncan, 37 Castle Court, 1 King's Gardens, Newton Mearns, Glasgow G77

Edinburgh Writers' Club
Contact: Mrs Margaret McArthur, 3 Craigcrook Road, Edinburgh EH14 3NQ

Elgin Writers
Contact: Mrs M. Totterdell, Grieve's Cottage, Ruthven, Huntly AB54 4SR

Erskine Writers' Workshop
Contact: Sheila Lewis, 94 Netherblane, Blanefield, Glasgow G63 9JP

Falkirk Writers' Circle
Contact: Mrs Isobel Quinn, 73 Alma Street, Falkirk FK2 7HE

Fife Writers' Group
Contact: Mr Sandy Latto, 58 Station Road, Thornton KY1 4AY

Galashiels Writers' Group
Contact: Mr Brian Mawhinney, 1 Bakery Cottage, Station Road, Chirnside, Duns TD11 3LJ

Garnethill Writers' Group
Contact: Mr Jack Crossan, Garnethill Community Centre, 21 Rose Street, Glasgow

Glasgow Eastern Writers' Association
Contact: Mr D. L. Bhatti, 50 Solway Road, Bishopbriggs, Glasgow G64 1QN

Greenock Writers' Club
Contact: Mrs Edith Sanders, 11 Welbeck Street, Greenock PA16 7RW

Helensburgh and District Writers' Club
Contact: Mrs Anne Mackintosh, 3 Glenan Gardens, West Argyle Street, Helensburgh G84 8XT

Inverness Writers' Group
Contact: Ms Rosemary Greenlaw, 23 Dalcroy Road, Croy, Inverness IV1 2PQ

Kelso Arts Appreciation Society
Contact: Mr Stewart Sanderson, Primside Mill Farmhouse, Yethom, Kelso

Kinlochbervie Writers' Group
Contact: Mr G. E. Monshall, West Shinness, by Lairg, Sutherland IV27 4DW

Kirkcaldy Women Writers

Contact: Mrs Margaret MacDougall, 48 Mid Street, Pathhead Village, Kirkcaldy KY1 2PN

Orkney Arts Society

Contact: Fiona Cumming, Bringagarth, Innertown, Stromness, Orkney KW16

Perthshire Writers' Group

Contact: Mrs Nanette Fleming, Craigard, Perth Road, Blairgowrie PH10 6EJ

Scottish Association of Writers

Contact: Pat Bingham, Rowan Cottage, Station Road, Garmouth IV32 7LZ

Ullapool Entertainments

Contact: Julia Campbell, 26 Vyner Place, Morefield, Ullapool IV26 2YR

Women Writing Southside

Contact: Valerie Clements, 518 Victoria Road, Glasgow G42 8BG

There are a number of magazines and journals published for both aspiring and established writers. Two which are published in Scotland are: *Writers News* and *Writing Magazine* (the editor of both is Richard Bell). Further details of both magazines can be obtained from:

PO Box 4
Nairn
IV12 4HU
Tel: 01667 454441
Fax: 01667 454401

BIBLIOGRAPHY

Those marked * are available from the SPA's resource library and can be consulted or borrowed by SPA members only. The library also stocks trade magazines such as *The Bookseller*, *Publishing News* and *Books Ireland*.

─────── BOOK TRADE INFORMATION ───────

*__Book Facts__ (Book Marketing Ltd, London, 1995)

__Books and the Consumer 1993__ (Book Marketing Ltd, London, 1993)

__Books as Gifts__ (Book Marketing Ltd, London)

__Books: The International Market 1992__ (Euromonitor, London, 1992)

__Bookselling in Britain 1992__ (Jordon & Sons Ltd, Bristol, 1992)

__Borrowing Books – Readership and Library Usage__ (Book Marketing Ltd, London, 1992)

__Britain's Book Publishing Industry 1991__ (Jordan & Sons Ltd, Bristol, 1991)

*Fishwick, Frank, __PA Book Trade Yearbook__ (Publishers Association, London, 1994)

__Ten Year Technology Forecast of Printing and Publishing 1991–2001__ (Pira, Leatherhead, 1991)

*__The Euromonitor Book Report 1993__ (Euromonitor, London, 1993)

__UK Printing and Publishing Statistics 1994__ (Pira, Leatherhead, 1994)

__UK Publishing__ (Key Note Publishers, Hampton)

__World Book Markets 1992__ (Euromonitor, London, 1992)

───── COPYRIGHT, CONTRACTS AND RIGHTS ─────

*Brown, Simon TD, __Contract Law in Scotland__ (Steedman Ramage WS, Edinburgh, 1993)

*Cavendish, JM and Pool, Kate, __Handbook of Copyright in British Publishing Practices__, 3rd edition (Cassell, London, 1993)

*Clark, Charles, __Publishing Agreements: A Book of Precedents__ (Butterworths, London, 1993)

*__Copyright, Design and Patents Act 1988__ (HMSO, London, 1988)

*Clark, Charles __et al Translation, Co-edition and Joint Venture Publishing Agreements__ (Butterworths, London, 1993)

*Davies, Gill, __Book Commissioning and Acquisition__ (Blueprint, London, 1995)

Flint, Michael F., __A User's Guide to Copyright__ (Butterworths, London, 1985)

Henry, Michael, *Publishing and Multimedia Law* (Butterworths, London, 1994)

Kennedy, Gavin, *The Perfect Negotiation* (Butterworths, London, 1994)

Legat, Michael, *Understanding Publishers' Contracts* (Robert Hale, London)

*McCracken, Richard and Gilbart, Madeleine, *Buying and Clearing Rights: Print, Broadcast and Multimedia* (Blueprint, London, 1995)

*Owen, Lynette, *Selling Rights* 2nd edition (Blueprint, London, 1994)

The Photographers' Guide to the 1988 Copyright Act (British Photographers' Liaison Committee, London, 1989)

Thorn, Eric A., *Understanding Copyright: A Practical Guide* (Jay Books, Tunbridge Wells, 1990)

Wall, Raymond A., *Copyright Made Easier* (ASLIB, London, 1993)

DESIGN

Briefing Designers (Arts Council of Great Britain, London, 1992)

Barlow, Geoff and Eccles, Simon, *Typesetting & Composition* 2nd edition (Blueprint, London, 1992)

*Colyer, Martin, *Commissioning Illustration* (Phaidon Press, London, 1990)

Martin, D., *An Outline of Book Design* (Blueprint, London, 1989)

McLean, Ruari, *The Thames and Hudson Manual of Typography* (Thames and Hudson, London, 1992)

Williams, Robin, *The Non-Designers Design Book* (Peachpit Press Inc, London, 1994)

Williamson, Hugh, *Methods of Book Design* (Yale University Press, New Haven, 1983)

DESKTOP PUBLISHING

Black, Alison, *Typefaces for Desktop Publishing: A User Guide* (Architecture, Design and Technology Press, London, 1990)

Cookman, Brian, *Desktop Design: Getting the Professional Look* (Blueprint, London,1990)

Desktop Publishing Commentary (Pira, Leatherhead, 10 issues per annum)

Dorner, Jane, *Writing on Disk* (John Taylor Book Ventures, Hatfield)

*Hewson, David, *Introduction to Desktop Publishing: A Guide to Buying and Using a Desktop Publishing System* (John Taylor Book Ventures, Hatfield, 1989)

Lang, Kathy, *The Writer's Guide to Desktop Publishing* (Academic Press, London, 1987)

*Miles, John, *Design for Desktop Publishing* (John Taylor Book
  Ventures, Hatfield, 1989)
Taylor, John and Heale, Shirley, *Editing for Desktop Publishing*
  (John Taylor Book Ventures, Hatfield, 1990)
*Wilson-Davies, Kirsty *et al*, *Desktop Publishing* 4th edition
  (Blueprint, London, 1991)
Worlock, Peter, *An Introduction to Desk Top Publishing*
  (Heinemann, London, 1987)

─────────────────DIRECTORIES─────────────────

**Association of British Directory Publishers* *(London, 1993)*
**Authors and Illustrators List* (National Book League, London, 1985)
**Clé Directory of the Irish Book World* (Dublin, 1991)
**Directory of Book Publishers' Distributors and Wholesalers
  1994* (The Booksellers Association, London, 1994)
**Directory of Bookseller Association Members* (The Booksellers
  Association, London, annual publication)
Directory of Information Sources in the United Kingdom (Aslib,
  London)
**Directory of Members' Services 1996* (Society of Freelance
  Editors and Proofreaders, London, 1996)
**Directory of Childrens Writers from Scotland* (Book Trust
  Scotland, Glasgow, 1988)
**Directory of Publishing: Continental Europe* (Cassell/The
  Publishers Association, London, 1993)
**Directory of Publishing Volume 1: United Kingdom* (Cassell/
  The Publishers Association, London, 1996)
**Directory of Specialist Children's Booksellers* (The Booksellers
  Association, London, 1991)
**Education Authorities Directory and Annual 1991* (School
  Government Publishing Co, Redhill, 1991)
*Harrold, Ann (ed), *Libraries in the United Kingdom and the
  Repubic of Ireland* (Library Association Publishing Ltd,
  London, 1992)
**Indexers Available* (Society of Indexers, London, 1996)
**Indexers Available in Scotland* (Society of Indexers, Gullane,
  1994)
**International Literary Marketplace* (Bowker Saur, London)
**Literary Marketplace* (Bowker Saur, London)
**Publishers in the UK and their Addresses 1993* (Whittaker,
  London, 1993)
**The Primary Education Directory* (School Government
  Publishing Co, Redhill)
**The Public Relations Yearbook 1994* (Public Relations
  Consultants Association, London, 1994)
**Register of US Book Importers* (Publishers Association,
  London, 1992)

*__Scottish Library and Information Resources__ (Scottish Library Association, Motherwell, 1996)
*__Small Press Yearbook 1992__ (Small Press Group of Great Britain, 1991)
__The European Book World__ (Anderson Rand, Cambridge, 1991)
__The Libraries Directory 1991–93__ (James Clarke & Co, Cambridge)
__Women in Publishing Directory 1990__ (Women in Publishing, London, 1989)

EDITING AND INDEXING

Bell, K. Hazel, __Indexing Biographies and other Stories of Human Lives__ (Society of Indexers, London, 1992)
Blake, Doreen __et al__, __Indexing the Medical and Biological Sciences__ (Society of Indexers, London 1995)
*Butcher, Judith, __Copy-editing – The Cambridge Handbook for Editors, Authors and Publishers__ 3rd edition (Cambridge University Press, 1992)
Carey, G.V., __Mind the Stop__ (Penguin, London, 1958
Davies, Gill, __Book Commissioning and Aquisition__ (Blueprint, London, 1994)
*Harris, Nicola, __Basic Editing: A Practical Course – The Exercises__ (Book House Training Centre/UNESCO, London, 1991)
*Harris, Nicola, __Basic Editing: A Practical Course – The Text__ (Book House Training Centre/UNESCO, London, 1991)
*__Hart's Rules for Compositors and Readers at the University Press, Oxford__ 39th edition (Oxford University Press, 1990)
*Knight, G. Norman, __Indexing, The Art of: A Guide to the Indexing of Books and Periodicals__ (Allen & Unwin, London, 1979)
Mulvany, C. Nancy, __Indexing Books__ (University of Chicago Press, Chicago and London, 1994)
__The Oxford Writers' Dictionary__ (Oxford University Press, 1990)
__The Oxford Dictionary for Writers and Editors__ (Oxford University Press, 1981)
Wellish, H. Hans, __Indexing from A to Z__ (H.H. Wilson, New York, 1991)

ELECTRONIC PUBLISHING

Blunden, Brian and Margot, edited by, __The Electronic Publishing Business and its Market__ (Blueprint, London, 1994)
Card, Michael and Feldman, Tony, __The Blueprint Electronic Publishing Glossary__ (Blueprint, London, 1991)
Ellsworth, Jill and Matthew, __Marketing on the Internet__ (John Wiley & Sons, Chichester, 1995)
*Feldman, Tony, __Multimedia__ (Blueprint, London, 1994)
Kennedy, Angus J. __The Internet & World Wide Web__ (Penguin, London, 1995)

FREELANCERS

A Directory of Speakers Available Under the ASLS Lecture Scheme (Association for Scottish Literary Studies, Aberdeen)

Indexers Available (The Society of Indexers, London)

Indexers Available in Scotland (The Society of Indexers, Gullane)

The National Union of Journalists Freelance Directory (National Union of Journalists, London)

The National Union of Journalists Freelance Fees Guide (National Union of Journalists, London)

The Society of Freelance Editors and Proofreaders Directory (SFEP, London)

GRANTS AND PRIZES

Guide to Literary Prizes, Grants and Awards (Book Trust, London, 1992)

The Arts Funding Guide (Directory of Social Change, London)

PICTURE RESEARCH

Evans, Hilary, *Practical Picture Research* (Blueprint, London, 1992)

Evans, Hilary and Mary, *Picture Researcher's Handbook* 5th edition (Blueprint, London, 1992)

PRODUCTION

*Bann, David, *The Print Production Handbook* (Macdonald Illustrated, London, 1985)

Bann, David, *Book Production Control* (Pira International, Leatherhead, 1995)

Barnard, Michael, *Introduction to Printing Processes* (Blueprint, London, 1991)

*Barnard, Michael *et al*, *The Blueprint Handbook of Print and Production* (Blueprint, London, 1994)

Barnard, Michael *et al, *The Pindar Pocket Print Production Guide* (Blueprint, London, 1995)

Birkenshaw, John, *Short Run Printing* (Pira, Leatherhead, 1994)

Book Production Practice (British Printing Industries Federation/Publishers Association, London, 1978)

Green, Phil, *Quality Control for Print Buyers* (Blueprint, London, 1992)

Johnson and Scott-Taggart, *Guidelines for Choosing the Correct Viewing Conditions for Colour Publishing* (Pira, Leatherhead, 1994)

Mortimer, Anthony, *Pira Guide to Colour Reproduction in the Printing Industry* (Pira, Leatherhead, 1991)

Publications for Printers (British Printing Industries Federation, 1993)

Publishing Technology Review (Pira, Leatherhead, 10 issues per annum)

*Peacock, John, **Book Production** (Blueprint, London, 1989)

The International Directory of Printers (Blueprint, London, 1993)

Print Price Guide (Ingram Publishing Ltd, Cheshire, 1995)

Scottish Print Directory (Scottish Print Employers Federation, Edinburgh, annual publication)

──────── PUBLICITY AND MARKETING ────────

*Baverstock, Alison, **Are Book Different? Marketing in the Book Trade** (Kogan Page, London, 1993)

*Baverstock, Alison, **How to Market Books** (Kogan Page, London, 1992)

Baverstock, Alison, **Commonsense Marketing for Non-Marketers** (Piatkus Books, London, 1995)

Bodian, Nat G., **Book Marketing Handbook – Tips and Techniques** (Bowker Saur, London,1980)

Bodian, Nat G., **Book Marketing Handbook Volume 2 – Over 1000 More Tips and Techniques** (Bowker Saur, London,1983)

Crompton, Alastair, **The Craft of Copywriting** (Arrow Business Books Ltd, London, 1993)

*Dickinson, Sarah, **How to Take on the Media** (Wiedenfeld & Nicholson, London, 1990)

Author Events – Impact and Effectiveness (Book Marketing Limited, London)

Book Promotion, Sales and Distribution: A Management Training Course (Book House Training Centre/UNESCO, London, 1991)

Benn's Media Directory UK/Europe/World (Benn Business Information, Tonbridge)

BRAD – Media Facts at Your Fingertips (Maclena Hunter Ltd, Barnet)

Godber, Bill, *et al*, **Marketing for Small Publishers** *(Pluto Press, London, 1992)*

Hollis Press and Public Relations Annual (Hollis, Sunbury-on-Thames)

Hollis Sponsorship and Donations Yearbook 1994 (Hollis Directories Ltd, Sunbury-on-Thames, 1994)

PIMS UK Media Directory (PIMS UK Ltd, London)

Public Relations Consultancy 1994 Yearbook (Public Relations Consultants Association, 1994)

*Smith, Keith, **Marketing for Small Publishers** (Interaction Imprint, London, 1990)

*Sutherland, Jon & Gross, Nigel, **Marketing in Action** (Pitman, London, 1991)

The Services and Facilities Guide to Corporate Events (Showcase Publications, London, 1990)

Willings Press Guide (Reed Information Services, East Grinstead, annual publication)

──────────────GENERAL PUBLISHING──────────────

Allan, Walter & Curwen, Peter, *Competition and Choice in the Publishing Industry* (The Institute of Economic Affairs, London, 1991)

Book Facts: An Annual Compendium 1991 (Book Marketing Limited, London, 1991)

Clark, Charles, *Inside Book Publishing: A Career Builder's Guide* 2nd edition (Blueprint, London,1994)

Collin, P. H., *Dictionary of Printing and Publishing* (Peter Collin Publishing Ltd, 1989)

*Competition and Choice in the Publishing Industry (The Institute of Economic Affairs, London, 1991)

Dick, Eddie, *Bookmaking: A Case Study of Publishing* (SFC Media Education)

Dorner, Jane, *Writing on Disc* (John Taylor Book Ventures, London, 1992)

Feather, John, *A History of British Publishing* (Routledge, London, 1991)

Fishwick, F., Dr, *Non-Net Books: Some Possible Consequences* (Cranfield School of Management, 1991)

Legat, Michael, *An Author's Guide to Literary Agents* (Robert Hale, London, 1995)

Legat, Michael, *The Writer's Rights* (A & C Black, London, 1995)

*Imprints in Time: A History of Scottish Publishers Past and Present (Merchiston Publishing, Edinburgh, 1991)

Lines, June, *Careers in Publishing and Bookselling* (Kogan Page, London, 1994)

Norrie, Ian, *Mumby's Publishing and Bookselling in the Twentieth Century* 6th edition (Bell & Hyman, 1982)

Owen, Peter, *Publishing Now* (Peter Owen, London, 1993)

*Peacock, John, *Multilingual Dictionary of Printing and Publishing Terms* (Blueprint, London, 1993)

*Pirates, Pigs and Perfect Love: Why Books Are Vital (Department of Arts and Libraries, Renfrew)

*Public Lending Right information (PLR, Cleveland)

Ward, Audrey and Philip, *The Small Publisher: A Manual and Case Histories* (Oleander Press, Cambridge, 1979)

──────────────WRITING──────────────

Barnard, Michael, *Making Electronic Manuscripts* (Blueprint, London, 1989)

Bell, Charlie, *The Writers Guide to Self-Publishing* (The Dragonfly Press, 1991)

Bolt, David, *The Author's Handbook* (Piatkus Books, 1986)

Finch, Peter, *How to Publish Your Own Poetry* (Allison & Busby, London, 1985)

*Glasgow Books and Writers of the Twentieth Century (Book Trust Scotland, Edinburgh, 1990)

Guide for Authors (Basil Blackwell Ltd, Oxford, 1985)

Hyland, Paul, *Getting into Poetry* (Bloodaxe Books, Newcastle-Upon-Tyne, 1992)

*Legat, Michael, *Dear Author* (Allison & Busby, London, 1989)

*Legat, Michael, *The Author's Guide to Publishing* (Robert Hale, London, 1987)

Legat, Michael, *Writing for Pleasure and Profit* (Robert Hale, London, 1986)

*The Bright Young Writers' Guide to Scottish Culture Nos. 1, 2 and 3 (Akros Publications, Edinburgh, 1994)

*The Society of Authors: What it is and What it Does (The Society of Authors, London)

*The Writers and Artists Yearbook (A. & C. Black, annual publication)

*Turner, Barry, *The Writer's Handbook* (Macmillan/PEN, London, annual publication)

UK Tax Guide for Authors (Ernst & Young, London)

*Writers Register 1995 (Scottish Arts Council, Edinburgh, 1995)

Book House Training Centre has a mail order service for books on publishing. To obtain the free Book Publishing Books *catalogue, telephone 0181 874 2718.*

ALPHABETICAL INDEX

COMPANY/SERVICE INDEX

Print/Production

Addison, Rosemary 75
Antony Rowe Ltd 89
Cromwell Press, The 90, **92**
David Fletcher Associates 74
Ipswich Book Company, The 89
Redwood Books 89, **91**
Rutherford, Jan 81
Scott, Ronnie 77

Project Management

Addison, Rosemary 75
David Fletcher Associates 74
Smith, Dorothy Mitchell 78

Promotion/Marketing

David Fletcher Associates 74
Rutherford, Jan 81

Proofreading

Addison, Rosemary 75
Blackadder, Kate 75
Christie, Margaret 75
Coventry, Charles S. 79 (Gaelic
  also)
Dougray, Debbie 76
Houston, Bill 76
Irving, Alison J. 76
McAra, Duncan 78
Pickering, Stephanie 77
Smith, Dorothy Mitchell 78

Proofreading: Foreign Language

Bowers, Alison (French and
  Spanish) 75

Readers

Addison, Rosemary 75
Blackadder, Kate 75

Research

Manson-Smith, Derek 77
McOwan, Rennie 79

Sales

Gregor, David 87
Pugh, Brian 87
Seol Ltd 87

Translation

Pickering, Stephanie 77 (French)

Typing/Secretarial

Spence, Linda 74

Wholesale

Bookspeed 88

Writing/Re-writing

Albury, David 74
David Williams Picture Library 86
Houston, Bill 76
Irving, Alison J. 76
Manson-Smith, Derek 77
McAra, Duncan 78
McOwan, Rennie 79
Pickering, Stephanie 77
Rutherford, Jan 81
Scott, Ronnie 77
Sumner, Adrian T. 78

Have we missed you out?

In publishing the *Directory*, it is our aim to include as much information and as many organisations connected with publishing in Scotland as possible. We strive to keep up-to-date in order to achieve our aim but sometimes we are not aware of companies or people missing. If you know of such a company, organisation or individual, or if you have any suggestions for improving this publication, please complete the form below and send it to:

Susanne Gilmour
Scottish Publishers Association
FREEPOST
Edinburgh
EH11 0NX

Name: _____

Address: _____

_____

Postcode: _____

Please give full details of company, individual or organisation which you feel should be included in the *Directory*:

_____

_____

_____

_____

_____

_____

_____

_____

_____

_____

Thank you for your help